STATESMEN WHO WERE NEVER PRESIDENT

Volume III
In the Miller Center Series on
Statesmen Defeated for President

Edited by

Kenneth W. Thompson

UNIVERSITY
PRESS OF
AMERICA

Lanham • New York • Oxford

The Miller Center

University of Virginia

Copyright © 1997 by
University Press of America,® Inc.
4720 Boston Way
Lanham, Maryland 20706

12 Hid's Copse Rd.
Cummor Hill, Oxford OX2 9JJ

Copublished by arrangement with
The Miller Center of Public Affairs,
University of Virginia

The views expressed by the author(s) of this publication do not necessarily represent the
opinions of the Miller Center. We hold to Jefferson's dictum that: "Truth is the proper and
sufficient antagonist to error, and has nothing to fear from the conflict, unless by human
interposition, disarmed of her natural weapons, free argument and debate."

Library of Congress Cataloging-in-Publication Data

ISBN: 0-7618-0894-9 (cloth: alk. ppr.)
ISBN: 0-7618-0895-7 (pbk: alk. ppr.)

TO

WILLIAM WEMPLE

Contents

I: The Passing of the Progressive Era

II: The Era of the Modern Presidency: Statesmen Who Fell Short

v

CONTENTS

III: Statesmen as the Conscience of Society

Preface

Statesmen Defeated for President is a three-part series that the Miller Center inaugurated with the publication of *Lessons from Defeated Presidential Candidates*. The unifying theme of that volume was the chronicle of American statesmen who gained their party's nomination but lost in the presidential election. They included Charles Evans Hughes in 1916, John W. Davis in 1924, Herbert Hoover and his 1932 campaign for reelection when he lost to Franklin D. Roosevelt, Wendell Willkie in 1940, Thomas Dewey in 1944 and 1948, Adlai Stevenson in 1952 and 1956, Hubert Humphrey in 1968, and Walter Mondale in 1984, among others. The volume explored qualities of the candidates, reasons for their defeat, their political objectives and goals, their strategy and tactics, and certain flaws that may have led to their defeat.

The second volume, *Statesmen Who Were Never President*, centers around the story of statesmen who in most cases lost their bid for the presidency without ever gaining their party's nomination. We drew on our colleague Merrill Peterson for insights on the Great Triumvirate: Clay, Calhoun, and Webster. Professor Ari Hoogenboom of Brooklyn College and the City University of New York helped us understand two prominent leaders from the Gilded Age. William Jennings Bryan and Robert La Follette were main figures who never gained the presidency in the Progressive Era. Estes Kefauver and Richard B. Russell Jr. stand out as leaders in the Senate, yet they never received the presidency. General George C. Marshall is sometimes referred to as second only to George Washington as soldier-statesman. Owen D. Young's quest for the presidency is described as the candidacy that never was.

Dumas Malone frequently asked visitors to the Miller Center the question, "Why do great men never become president?" It is a question that can be asked about some of the candidates in volumes I and II of our series. The current volume continues the search for an answer to Malone's question. We hope others will pursue the question using whichever method is deemed appropriate to their ends.

Introduction

Professor John J. Broesamle is the author of a brilliant paper on William Gibbs McAdoo, the son-in-law of Woodrow Wilson. In one source it is a model of analysis for our series on *Statesmen Defeated for President*. His contribution reminds us, as do several others in this volume, that someone revered for his teaching can also be a major figure in research and writing. McAdoo, who was secretary of the treasury in the Wilson administration and later senator from California, appeared to have many of the qualities essential to the presidency. He was not only the most prominent Democrat in 1920 but the Framer of the Federal Reserve system and the overseer of the financing of a great world war. He also possessed some of the textbook qualities often cited for the presidency. He joined pragmatism with opportunism and political astuteness. He was a hero of organized labor and an early feminist. In Lippmann's words, "He was a statesman grafted upon a promoter." Why, then, did he fail? It would be a disservice for the editor to provide a summary of some of the reasons if it discouraged a single reader from reading Professor Broesamle's paper. Not to read it is to deprive oneself of the rare privilege of enjoying political analysis at its best and discovering the answer to a question that undergirds and is the purpose of the paper, namely, why McAdoo did not become president.

If Broesamle enables us to see why one of the great secretaries of the treasury and an acknowledged statesman failed to become president in the last years of the Progressive Era, Professor David Healy of the University of Wisconsin in Milwaukee does the same with James G. Blaine, who sought the highest office in the Gilded Age. His name was brought forward in five Republican nominating conventions. He in fact was—and in this he stands apart from the majority of statesmen in volumes one and two—the candidate nominated by the Republican Party for the presidency in 1884. He reshaped the Republican Party after the Civil War as the party of industrialization and economic growth. He stood out among the leaders of his age for knowledge of foreign policy and, especially in the Harrison administration, its practice. Why, then, did he fail? Was it the ill health from which he suffered increasingly over the years? Was he too long unsuccessful, too much the candidate of those who were his passionate followers, arrayed against too many who hated him? What are the facts regarding charges of corruption and in this respect his being the symbol of the Gilded Age? Why have there been revisionist views among historians who portray him in a more favorable light? These are some of the issues surrounding his political career that help to explain his failures to gain the presidency. Professor Healy is tireless in his resolve to portray a full picture of Blaine's long quest for the office, and as with the Broesamle essay, he merits a dedicated readership.

A half century elapsed from the 1880s to the 1930s. The 1930s ushered in the modern presidency. It became the age of Franklin D. Roosevelt but also of challengers such as Taft, Landon, and Willkie. Robert A. Taft was Mr. Republican for many Americans, but he failed in four attempts to gain the presidency. His father was William Howard Taft, who was president from 1908 to 1912. The father was considered a Progressive president. The son was a favorite son candidate from Ohio in 1936. When it was clear that Alf Landon, the father of Kansas senator Nancy Kassebaum, had gained an early lead, Taft withdrew and joined others in seconding Landon's nomination. His two most bitter campaigns for the Republican nomination were in 1944 and 1948 against Governor Thomas Dewey of New York. His greatest disappointment was 1952. These campaigns pitted earlier internationalism against Midwest isolationism. The contest involved two wings of the Republican Party with centers in New York and Ohio. Congressman Clarence Brown of Ohio was Taft's campaign manager, and Herbert Brownell, who had served in the New York legislature, ran Dewey's campaign.

No one questioned Taft's intellectual strengths and his stature. He served in the Senate from 1938 until his death in 1953. In those

15 years, he earned the reputation of skilled legislator and a true student of government. Despite his devotion to conservatism, his views on social legislation, including public health measures, were more liberal than those who defeated him, especially Dwight D. Eisenhower. At the same time he is remembered for certain conservative legislation, such as the Taft-Hartley Act, which banned the secondary boycott of labor unions.

If Taft never gained the presidency, his failures can hardly be attributed to lack of knowledge, nor his having committed supporters and party organizers. Rather, he suffered because he gave the impression of being remote and aloof from his constituents and the people. In a sense, he was too much the scholar and thinker. He also spoke his mind whatever the political consequences. He ferreted out the last detail in his research on the problems he addressed in legislation and speeches. He was the author of various health plans, especially later in his career. He was said to be a regional candidate because he appeared to represent primarily Ohio and certain states in the Midwest, not the country as a whole, a judgment his supporters acknowledged. He was anything but an inspiring speaker. He appeared almost dyspeptic and chronically ill. It was tempting to stereotype his thinking when in fact his views were often intricate and complex. For example, he opposed NATO at one stage in his foreign policy views, arguing that fundamentally, U.S. security depended on the nuclear deterrent rather than troops in Europe. Perhaps he lost out because New York bankers and financiers were more powerful than Ohio bankers. Those who surrounded him were no match for the Dulleses, Brownells, and McCloys of the East.

Whatever the reason, he failed four times to gain the nomination and the presidency despite his extraordinary talents as a legislator and a thinker. Many saw contradictions in him with his rather powerful physique (he was a large man) combined with a characteristically pale and emaciated appearance. He had unquestioned intellectual powers, but they were combined with his seeming confusion on simplifying and popularizing complex issues. He was far more concerned with the fate of hard-pressed poor people than he received credit for being, perhaps because he framed his decisions primarily in economic terms, leaving the impression that he was indifferent to human problems. He was a relentless debater, as in his campaign for the Senate in 1950. His compassion and concern were obscured by his intellectual virtuosity. In Ohio, he was virtually unbeatable, but he failed to receive the presidential nomination from the national Republicans. Those closest to him admired him, but he had an aversion to shaking hands and engaging in small talk. He ridiculed the world federalists but favored world government in speeches immediately after World War II. As Mr. Wemple has pointed out, Taft might have gained the presidency in different times and different circumstances, but we shall never know.

Senator Mike Mansfield deserves a thoughtful and skilled chronicler, and Gregory Olson performs that role. Particularly concerned with rhetoric and communications, Professor Olson turns out to be a well-qualified scholar and penetrating analyst of domestic and international politics. He provides an authoritative and nuanced appraisal of Mansfield that builds on an extensive oral history by Frank Valeo. Those who lived through the 1960s remember Mansfield as an independent force in the Senate who sought through educating himself about Vietnam to educate other decisionmakers and the public. Sometimes devoid of signs of ego and given to a laconic and low-keyed style, he was an outstanding majority leader for almost two decades. Olson explores Mansfield's goals and ambitions and concludes that he probably never seriously considered a run for the presidency or vice presidency but adds a couple of caveats. He was whip in 1956 and majority leader from 1961 to 1976, longer than any leader in history. In 1956, he was mentioned as a possible Catholic running mate for Adlai Stevenson. Again in 1964, just before the convention, Johnson from a mixture of motives used journalist William White to send up a trial-balloon rumor, but Mansfield told the President that he would not accept. Again in 1972, George McGovern approached Mansfield, who once more declined the honor. From the Senate Historical Office, Olson received a copy of their 900-page interview with Frank Valeo, who was Mansfield's principal aide. It confirmed Olson's judgment about Mansfield's reluctance toward the vice presidency, but Valeo accompanied him to the convention in 1964. Since Mansfield has rarely attended previous nominating conventions, Valeo could only conclude that he was there to draft an acceptance speech if the vice presidency was offered. From this and other comments, Valeo apparently concluded that Mansfield may have been interested in the vice presidency or at least was ambivalent. Valeo's view, however, was the exception to the general impression that Mansfield was not interested in either of the top presidential offices. Olson concludes that Mansfield is to Montana what La Follette is to Wisconsin and Hubert Humphrey is to Minnesota.

Randall Bennett Woods is a respected historian at the University of Arkansas and is known particularly for his publications in international relations. His book, *The Dawning of the Cold War: America's Quest for Order, 1945–1950*, is cited by students of American foreign policy. He recounts some of the main events in Fulbright's early life, including the influence his mother exerted in his appointment as a Rhodes scholar and as president of the University of Arkansas. His family was a major force in business and in managing their newspaper. He grew up in the northwestern part of the state in which blacks comprised less than 2 percent of the population. In this environment, Fulbright absorbed an attitude toward race that was to stand in the way of his appointment as secretary of state in the Kennedy administration. As a Rhodes scholar, he traveled in Eastern Europe, and this environment started him on the road to a major interest in foreign policy. That interest culminates in his being chosen chairman of the Senate Foreign Relations Committee. He had grown up as a member of a provincial aristocracy in Arkansas, and Democrat that he was, an air of the aristocrat continued to mark his demeanor through the rest of his career. Early in his senatorial career, he favored the supremacy of the executive in foreign policy, but dismay over Vietnam and his own experience led to the view that Congress was as essential in foreign as in domestic policy. He came close to making the Senate Foreign Relations Committee an alternative State Department. He had run for Congress in 1942, defeated the race-baiting governor who had fired him as president of the University of Arkansas in a race for the Senate in 1944 and sponsored legislation creating the Fulbright Exchange Program in 1946. That program was to be his pride in life and his monument in death. He was a conventional internationalist in the 1940s, supporting the

Marshall Plan and the Truman Doctrine. His anticommunism was more that of George Kennan and containment than NSC-68, but he voted against every civil rights measure that came before Congress until 1970, making his reputation with the liberal community ambiguous. He was disdainful of the Eisenhower administration and especially John Foster Dulles, but he came to appreciate it more in his later years. His Senate hearing on Vietnam attracted nationwide attention. He was emotionally and psychologically unable to do what was necessary to become president and perhaps too lazy.

Lee R. Powell is the author of another biography on Senator Fulbright. In its first pages, he reveals that almost alone among prominent senators, Fulbright had no presidential ambitions. Columnist Dorothy Thompson in early 1945 had written of him as a man of presidential timber. He was the unanimous choice of a faculty committee for the presidency of Columbia University before General Eisenhower was appointed. As a young congressman, he had sponsored a resolution placing the country on record as supporting its participation in the United Nations. His foreign policy reputation was outstanding, but his civil rights record was an insuperable obstacle to his becoming president. He lacked the necessary ambition, did not suffer fools, and Arkansas as a power base was at the time too small. Powell examines the criticism that he was incapable of pushing a legislative program through Congress and offers evidence to the contrary. At the same time, he acknowledges that the senator was often a dissenter. He was a leader of immense courage, and Powell provides examples. The main difference between Randall Wood's and Lee Powell's chapters has to do with whether Fulbright was a racist. Powell includes a quotation from Wood's biography of Fulbright which asserts that Fulbright indisputably was a racist. Powell finds this statement the most superficial ever written about Fulbright. He admits, however, that he could have gone further than he did in opposing segregationists in Arkansas and cites as an example the Little Rock Central High School crisis in 1957. Powell concludes with Wood that Fulbright probably served the country better from his pulpit in the Senate than he would have done as a president hampered by his civil rights record and was stronger as a dissenter than as a coalition builder and molder of public opinion. Mr. Powell answers a broad range of questions in the last third of his presentation.

Senator John McCain of Arizona is a moderate Republican. His courage as a prisoner of war in Vietnam and his independent political views have captured the imagination of the nation. His co-sponsorship of a major campaign finance reform bill, the Feingold-McCain bill, has drawn support from unexpected quarters. McCain's address at the Republican national convention was a high point in the proceedings. The Senator recounts that any time he is in Phoenix, he goes to see Morris Udall. He describes Mo Udall as the true conscience of the nation. Although Udall is dying of Parkinson's disease, he sometimes appears to recognize McCain. McCain considers his brief moment with Udall on his visit to his home state a mountain-peak experience; that is, until his next visit. Others speak in a similar vein of their feelings about Udall. His brother, Stewart Udall, was invited to conduct an oral history interview concerning his brother. As it turned out, he combined the oral history with a discussion of his all-consuming interest in the environment movement. The two topics are not unrelated. Mo Udall was also interested in the environment. Together, the Udalls called for a national crusade to solve the more pressing environmental problems. The fact that others have continued the crusade provides further evidence that Mo Udall was a statesman. His illness and the fact that he was more interested in conscience-building than coalition-building prevented him from doing more. Yet from a moral standpoint, he left his imprint.

Senator Edmund Muskie deserves inclusion in any volume on American statesmen. Although he was a candidate for vice president in Hubert Humphrey's 1968 campaign for the presidency, Muskie never received the Democratic Party nomination for the presidency. Prize-winning author Bernard Asbell tells the story in a remarkable book entitled *The Senate Nobody Knows*. Some people have called the book the best case study available on the U.S. Congress in action. It tracks Senator Muskie's efforts in ushering the Clean Air Act through the Senate. Asbell was allowed complete access to Muskie activities and he describes the senator's novel strategy in shepherding the bill through the Congress. He developed a theory called "forced technology," which mandates that motor cars must reduce pollution by 90 percent in five years without requiring that any particular technology or technique be adopted. A critical aspect of Muskie's strategy was first to discover "the disagreement" and then work from there. He collaborated with Senator James Buckley on the legislation and with others from both parties. I had the good fortune of working with Senator Muskie on the Miller Center's Commission on the Selection of Vice Presidents. He was co-chairman of the commission and played a decisive role in bringing about consensus. Senator Muskie was an inspiration to all who served with him whatever the endeavor. His commitment to public service was exemplary.

Cary Reich is the author of a magisterial biography of Nelson A. Rockefeller that not only reflects prodigious research but also a sense of Rockefeller as a person. The first volume covers the formative period in Rockefeller's life from 1908 to 1958 and the second continues through the rest of his life. Rockefeller was the most vital and dynamic of five extraordinary brothers. It would be difficult to overestimate the contribution that each of them made to the well-being of mankind. Yet Nelson was continually in the public eye. He served in several administrations, was vice president in Gerald Ford's abbreviated term, and was mentioned for president several times. He had unlimited resources, vast contacts at home and abroad, and was an internationally recognized leader. Was his wealth both an asset and a liability in his quest for the office? Were his strengths better adapted to his many private nonprofit activities and to his four-term governorship than to national politics? He lost key advisers like Frank Jamieson just at the point when he embarked on his campaign for the presidency. Vietnam had occurred as he sought the office in 1964. So far as the presidency was concerned, the environment was not propitious for a liberal like Rockefeller. How harmed was he by a highly publicized divorce and the fact that his second wife bore him a child at the time of the Republican convention? Rockefeller was the leader of the eastern wing of the party, which may also have made his quest more difficult. The Rockefeller story is one deserving of the extraordinary talents of Cary Reich.

I

THE PASSING OF
THE PROGRESSIVE ERA

CHAPTER ONE

William Gibbs McAdoo and the Hopeless Candidacy Syndrome*

JOHN J. BROESAMLE

NARRATOR: John J. Broesamle is professor of history at California State University at Northridge. He received his bachelor's degree from the University of the Pacific and his master's and doctorate degrees from Columbia University. In addition to having more than 25 years of teaching experience, he is the author of several significant books, including *William Gibbs McAdoo: A Passion for Change, 1863-1917* (1973), *Reform and Reaction in Twentieth Century American Politics* (1990), and *Suddenly a Giant: A History of California State University, Northridge* (1993). Professor Broesamle has also written important articles and book chapters on such subjects as the Democratic Party in the Progressive Era, the workings of the Federal Reserve system, and cross-cultural perspectives in history. He is currently writing a novel on academic life.

Professor Broesamle has received numerous honors and awards for his research. He was a Woodrow Wilson Fellow from 1964 to 1965 and then a Woodrow Wilson Dissertation Fellow from 1966 to 1967. He was awarded several institutional fellowships at Columbia University, and he became a Danforth Associate in 1981.

Presented in a Forum at the Miller Center of Public Affairs on 13 September 1996.

In addition to his experience in academia, Professor Broesamle has served as vice president of the Ojai Valley Land Conservancy, the community in which he and his wife currently reside.

As I read Professor Broesamle's remarkable book about Secretary McAdoo, I was intrigued by this exceptional man's little-noted bids for the presidency. Although William Gibbs McAdoo was secretary of the treasury in the Wilson administration, few remember his attempts to gain the presidency. His quest and what it can explain about the American political system are the subjects of Professor Broesamle's paper today.

MR. BROESAMLE: It seems strange that William Gibbs McAdoo never secured the Democratic Party's nomination for president. As Douglas B. Craig has said, "Apart from Woodrow Wilson, William Gibbs McAdoo was the most prominent Democrat in the United States in 1920. . . . McAdoo, it seemed, was the great success story of the [Wilson] administration." As a shaper of the new Federal Reserve system and the overseer of World War I financing, McAdoo had been one of the genuinely great secretaries of the treasury. Yet the decade of the 1920s proved as disastrous to McAdoo's ambitions for the Democratic presidential nomination as it did to his party's hopes for retaining or recapturing the presidency. Part of the difficulty had to do with McAdoo himself. The other part was quite beyond his control. Behind McAdoo's career lies one of the strangest, most bewildering tales in American political history.

McAdoo ranks near the top among 20th-century second-echelon American political figures—arguably even among the lower level of the first echelon. He was a man who combined enormous vitality with a distinctly southern kind of gentility. Born in 1863 near Marietta, Georgia, he grew up in a region devastated by the Civil War and in a family declassed by it. Unsurprisingly, during future years, money would never lie far from McAdoo's mind. After spending three years at the University of Tennessee he went to Chattanooga to study law. He became a lawyer-promoter, first in the South and then, after 1892, in New York City. It was his company that built the subway tunnels under the Hudson River that connected New York to New Jersey. He was an odd fellow—a New

4

York business executive suspicious of Wall Street and with a bent toward social justice, particularly the welfare of women and children. This made him that rare sort of businessman whom Woodrow Wilson lionized in his New Freedom campaign of 1912. McAdoo became Wilson's de facto campaign manager in that election. When Wilson won, he named McAdoo secretary of the treasury.

The former college professor who believed in the idea of an unmerciful god and the railroad promoter-turned-politician were not exactly ideally matched. Once at a White House luncheon, for example, Wilson asked McAdoo to say the blessing. McAdoo stood up, but he could not utter a single word. Finally blurting out "Jesus," he abruptly sat down again. One-word graces did not pass muster in the Wilson household. McAdoo's wife—who happened to be Wilson's daughter—coached her husband on how to say grace, but apparently it did not take. McAdoo had to crib his next blessing by reading notes off the cuff of his shirt.

Being at a loss for words was rare for McAdoo. His sense of humor (unlike so many politicians today, he did have one) extended toward storytelling and practical jokes. Along with being funny, he could be enormously persuasive. He was a natural salesman and he attracted a political following that became wildly devoted to him. McAdoo was a pragmatist—without delving into Dewey or James, he followed the gospel of doing what works. "I do not like ideas that are suspended in the air," he wrote. "There is not much metaphysics in my temperament."

McAdoo fused pragmatism with political astuteness. At the outset of 1918, the federal government took over the railroads as a wartime expedient with McAdoo in charge as commissioner. In that role he guaranteed collective bargaining rights and hiked some wages more than 40 percent. An outspoken feminist, he ordered equal pay for equal work for women as well as blacks. McAdoo was an early 20th-century hero of organized labor.

Often the underside of pragmatism is opportunism, which McAdoo epitomized more aggressively than any major figure of the Wilson administration. Following his Cabinet appointment, the man whom many regarded as a paragon of practical Progressivism increasingly revealed this other side. Walter Lippmann characterized him as "a statesman grafted upon a promoter." This characterization was neither completely fair to McAdoo nor altogether wrong. His promoter's opportunism ultimately helped to undo his presidential aspirations during the 1920s.

Ironically, his father-in-law, President Wilson, also helped to undo him. In 1919 Wilson was devastated by a stroke that nearly killed him. The Democrats had lost control of both houses of Congress in 1918. Even so, the stricken Wilson wanted the 1920 Democratic national convention to draft him. Wilson's acceptance speech was written and waiting. Of 1,094 delegates, exactly two gave Wilson their votes.

Wilson's illusions became a disaster for McAdoo. McAdoo bore the sobriquet (or epithet) "Crown Prince" of the Wilson administration. He had plenty of momentum toward the nomination and could probably have gotten it, but he could not run against his father-in-law, the sitting Democratic president. Instead, from 1919 to early 1920 he waited for Wilson to endorse him, or at least to get out of the way. Meanwhile, McAdoo's campaign remained hamstrung. As Burl Noggle has stated in his book, *Into the Twenties: The United States from Armistice to Normalcy* (1974), "Wanting to run, McAdoo was stymied at every turn." A key difficulty involved his participation in the primaries. Early in 1920 McAdoo wrote the following to an important backer: "I do not want to enter these primaries and I am greatly puzzled about them. If I refuse to allow my name to be used it will be assumed that I would, in no circumstances, go into the race, [and yet] I am not prepared to eliminate myself completely." Instead, he would "wait until conditions are clearer." Unfortunately, the fog absolutely refused to lift.

McAdoo tried another tack. Requesting that his name not be entered in the Georgia primary, he telegraphed: "I cannot consistently enter the primary in any state when it is my earnest conviction that the delegate from every state should go to the Convention without instruction." Loosely translated, this statement meant that he could not publicly seek nomination, so he should be drafted at an open convention. Or as McAdoo himself put it in correspondence, "It would be my duty to accept the nomination if it came to me unsolicited." This statement suggested avoiding a public campaign while expanding support privately and hoping for the best when the Democrats gathered late in June in San Francisco.

Ten days before the convention, fearful of alienating Wilson, McAdoo pulled out of the race, or so it seemed. He declared that he would not permit his name to be put before the convention. Even then a real chance for a nomination remained. As Wilson himself remarked to one senator, McAdoo had not actually issued a General Sherman statement. Having given one withdrawal declaration, McAdoo indicated that he would not release a second. Quipped the Chicago *Tribune*, "Mr. McAdoo wishes us all distinctly to understand that if the San Francisco convention does not offer him the nomination, he will not accept it." In the wake of his withdrawal statement, much of his support dispersed. Even so, McAdoo led on the first 11 convention ballots, fell behind to conservative Ohio governor James M. Cox, then pulled ahead again on ballot 29 before eventually fading. On the 44th round, Cox finally took the nomination. "By his enigmatic role," writes William E. Leuchtenburg in *The Perils of Prosperity: 1914–1932* (1993), "Wilson [had] destroyed the political hopes of the party's one attractive candidate."

    However broad McAdoo's appeal may have been, though, the very threat of a McAdoo candidacy did upset important elements in the Democratic Party, notably bosses such as Charles Murphy of New York, George Brennan of Illinois, and Tom Taggart of Indiana. The anti-McAdoo faction regarded McAdoo as too close to Wilson and the unpopular League of Nations issue. Apparently most urbanites distrusted McAdoo, who backed the 18th (prohibition) Amendment. Finally, McAdoo had something of a reputation as a radical. He disdained Wall Street and had a myriad of enemies in business, industry, railroads, and banking. His railroad record during World War I told the tale. McAdoo had run a temporarily nationalized transportation system, bestowed major gains upon organized labor much to the distress of management, and clearly wanted nationalization to continue for an extended period after the war. Conservative elements in the party could plainly see that McAdoo's backers were southerners and westerners who, before becoming Wilsonians, had been the Bryanites whom conservatives had despised and feared. Governor Cox, a self-made millionaire, was the choice of anti-McAdoo bosses and the party's business-oriented conservatives. To complete the ticket, the vice-presidential nod went to McAdoo's onetime anti-Tammany ally in New York politics, the affable and charming Franklin D. Roosevelt. Cox and Roosevelt lost by a large margin to Warren G. Harding.

By 1920, the Democratic Party was falling into dilapidation and decay. Wilson's two victories in 1912 and 1916 had represented an aberration based upon a short-term Democratic revival during the Progressive Era and a Republican split in 1912. World War I and the resultant peace treaties had angered key ethnic constituencies— the Germans because the United States had fought Germany, the Irish because the United States had sided with Britain, and the Italians because of a disappointing peace settlement for Italy. Domestic problems may have played an even more damaging role. Resentment had built up against wartime regulations, together with raging inflation, Wilson's farm policies, postwar unemployment, and a wave of strikes in 1919. The Democrats' popularity was in decline. In general, Democrats who had a southern or western base in the party lost influence as the 1920s advanced. One of these was William G. McAdoo, whose candidacy in 1924 looked significantly different from the candidacy of four years earlier.

Most historians consider McAdoo the cause of his own undoing in 1924. Ambition and expediency, the argument goes, outran judgment. The two key facts can be briefly stated. First, the Teapot Dome oil scandal tarred McAdoo because he had taken a big retainer from oil magnate Edward L. Doheny. Second, in the midst of the ethnic and cultural struggles of the 1920s, McAdoo accepted support from the Ku Klux Klan.

In the face of Tammany opposition, New York was an impossible place from which to launch a presidential candidacy. It was also not a logical base for a candidate in the Bryan-Wilson mold. In 1922 McAdoo began practicing law in Los Angeles. "While developing a general practice in California," he cheerfully wrote, "I'd have the advantage of one client at the start." That client was Edward L. Doheny. McAdoo accepted $50,000 from Doheny as counsel to negotiate with the government of Mexico over its intention to expropriate Doheny's Pan-American Petroleum

Company holdings. In the meantime, McAdoo retained his original identity as a labor candidate and a Progressive. He was also a favorite of prohibitionists. With this sheer breadth of support, McAdoo was easily the Democratic front-runner for 1924. Then things began to unravel. In February 1924, Woodrow Wilson died, and with him the possibility of an endorsement. The site chosen for the Democratic national convention was New York—"an environment naturally hostile to me," McAdoo accurately complained, "so far as big business and Wall Street influence is concerned." Since the party's venerable two-thirds rule remained in effect, actually taking the nomination meant winning not a simple majority, but two-thirds of the convention delegates. New York governor Al Smith and others got into the race, making two-thirds a difficult stretch. Then the Teapot Dome scandal broke.

After Doheny admitted that he had bribed the secretary of the interior to get access to naval oil reserves in Wyoming, he also made public the fact that he had retained McAdoo as counsel. McAdoo had connections with Mexican oil, but none to Teapot Dome. All the same, his activities took on an odor of guilt, partly by association and partly because McAdoo's law firm could ultimately have made around a million dollars out of the deal. These revelations, together with others about McAdoo's having argued cases before the Treasury Department shortly after his resignation as secretary of the treasury, raised questions about character and judgment reminiscent of Whitewater. How could Democrats attack Republicans over a Republican scandal if a man tied to Doheny headed the Democratic ticket? McAdoo was widely written off as a political corpse. Some railway unions, for instance, had wanted McAdoo until Teapot Dome, but they then broke away toward a third party.

The unions' departure illustrates the way in which Progressivism fell apart in the 1920s. McAdoo's model for the Democratic Party involved reviving Wilsonian reform program around not only Wilson's 1916 electoral coalition of West and South, but also around farmers, workers, and veterans. This vision placed him well to the left of any other leading Democratic candidate. McAdoo specifically wanted reduced influence for big banks in the Federal Reserve system, ratification of a child labor amendment to the Constitution,

9

steeply graduated income taxes, high inheritance taxes, other methods of income redistribution, dramatically lowered tariff rates, and increased Interstate Commerce Commission authority. In short, McAdoo supported an activist government building upon the Wilsonian model. These proposals, together with McAdoo's record of harshness toward certain banks and corporations in the Cabinet, generated, in Edward M. House's words, an "intense antagonism" to McAdoo's candidacy from business that was comparable to its earlier hostility to Bryan.

After Doheny's revelations, McAdoo was irate. One political intimate described him as "mad. He is full of fight. He is swearing mad. He is . . . profane. . . . He is cursing and swearing, damning every opponent and every obstacle." Though others wrote off his chances, McAdoo launched himself into the primaries. Despite the storm around his candidacy, he got just under 60 percent of the 1924 primary vote. He entered the convention with more pledged delegates than any other candidate. Strongest in the South, he was the clear favorite of prohibitionists, who supported him solidly. He also held onto Progressives and labor from the South and West. Finally, he had the backing of two-thirds or more of those cozy with the Ku Klux Klan. No less than the Imperial Wizard of the KKK, Hiram Evans, endorsed him. Disregarding plenty of morally sound advice against accepting Klan support in favor of transparent political calculation, McAdoo was the only major candidate going into the convention who had failed to denounce the KKK.

His calculation reflected broader realities. The United States was passing through an identity trauma during the 1920s as it transformed from a rural nation to an urban one. The decline of Jeffersonian-agrarian America, the massive impact of the "new" immigration, and the very allure of the city itself to the sons and daughters of the same country and small-town folk who had denounced it conspired massively to destabilize the political system by the mid-1920s. The struggle between country and city focused in the Democratic Party, where every word and action was redolent with cultural symbolism. Claiming to stand for the older America now being displaced, the Ku Klux Klan reached its apogee of power between 1920 and 1925. It more or less dominated the politics of half a dozen states. Harry Truman briefly flirted with it. Hugo

Black, Alabama senator from 1927 to 1937 and Supreme Court Justice until 1971, belonged to it.

McAdoo did not. He was not anti-Catholic. He had outspokenly opposed the oppression of Jews. On the other hand, his record on race was mixed. As railroad administrator during World War I, he had ordered equal pay for blacks. But before then he had taken a prominent part in an unprecedented event—the official segregation of the federal government by the administration of Woodrow Wilson. Though not a rabid racist, little that McAdoo said or did suggested that he thought blacks and whites were equal. Just as he appears to have espoused prohibition primarily because the regions that supported him wanted it rather than from deep personal convictions, his lack of convictions on civil rights made it easier for him to bow to the Klan.

Although he led in pledged delegates at convention time, McAdoo had only 270 of these; 732 were required to win the nomination. McAdoo knew that this number lay beyond his reach, but he thought that he could win with a majority if he could kill the two-thirds rule by pursuing the following plan. First, the McAdoo forces would use the rule to block other candidates. Then, with the convention deadlocked, the right "psychological moment" (his words) would arrive; McAdoo delegates would call for dropping the two-thirds rule; if the chair ruled against them, they would use their delegate majority to override him; and McAdoo would be the nominee.

Meanwhile, McAdoo engaged in some minor theatrics. Stepping off the train that brought him to New York, he immediately condemned the city as "reactionary, sinister, unscrupulous, mercenary, and sordid." This picture was precisely how rural towns such as South Bend or Paducah visualized New York. One would hardly have realized from his rhetoric that for 30 years before moving to Los Angeles, McAdoo had actually been a New Yorker.

On 24 June 1924, the convention opened at the old Madison Square Garden. The Barnum and Bailey Circus, an event not much different from this one, had recently left. Animal smells still lingered. Temperatures on the floor ran as high as 100 degrees. For the first time, radio broadcast the proceedings nationwide. "Every shade of opinion, every prejudice, every fear, every division which could be found in American society as a whole was duplicated in Madison Square Garden in 1924," writes Robert K. Murray in his book, *The 103rd Ballot: Democrats and the Disaster in Madison Square Garden* (1976). "In that struggle, which involved competing life styles, religious beliefs, social backgrounds, and conflicting moralities, partisan candidates like Smith and McAdoo elicited a fanatical response and became symbols which helped perpetuate and intensify that struggle." Much liquor was flowing. McAdoo apologized for breaching prohibition by eating sherry-soaked cake. He also complained that Al Smith supporters were keeping numerous McAdoo delegates inebriated: "Some of my best men have been hopelessly drunk ever since they landed in New York." Police had to prevent Ku Klux Klansmen in the Texas delegation from burning a cross outside Madison Square Garden.

An overriding issue involved whether or not to censure the Klan by name. This issue resembled the abortion question in the Republican Party today, a battle-axe that politicians saw swinging straight toward their heads. McAdoo wanted to dodge it, but the Smith backers, using it as a wedge issue, demanded that the convention condemn the KKK explicitly by name. McAdoo resisted. The upshot, after brawling, fistfights, and police intervention, was a vote of 541 and 3/20, to 542 and 3/20, to let the Klan escape. Crowed Imperial Wizard Evans: "They were afraid of what we might do." Predictably, a high correlation materialized between Klan support and McAdoo support. As Murray notes, "The Klan struggle not only made McAdoo and Smith victories all the more impossible, but made each of their camps all the more intransigent." Lost in the melee was the fact that besides the Klan, others backed McAdoo, including many Catholics, many Progressives, and financier Bernard Baruch.

The balloting opened on 30 June. It went on and on: 10, 20, 30, 40, 50 tallies. It was William G. McAdoo versus Al Smith, otherwise phrased as old stock Americans versus new, the rural South and West versus the urban Northeast, or the drys versus the wets. As David Burner writes in *The Politics of Provincialism: The Democratic Party in Transition, 1918–1932* (1968), "The deadlock that developed might as well have been a political contest between the Pope and the Imperial Wizard of the Klan, so solidly did the

Catholic delegates support Smith and the Klansmen support McAdoo." Tammany worked to stretch out the balloting so that rising hotel bills would drive their antagonists out of town. Packed with Smith supporters, the galleries shouted "Oil!" or "Al!" McAdoo tried to get the convention moved, to no avail. Quipped Will Rogers: "This thing has got to come to an end. New York invited you people here as guests, not to live."

At 58 ballots the convention set a record. It then slogged through 60, 70, and 80 ballots. On the 99th ballot, Smith and McAdoo were perfectly tied. McAdoo then released his delegates. By now the nomination was worthless. On the 103rd ballot, which occurred 13 days into the convention, the delegates finally nominated Wall Street lawyer John W. Davis, whose firm provided counsel to J. P. Morgan and Company. Balancing the ticket (to the point of parody) was Charles W. Bryan, William Jennings's prairie-radical brother. Faced with this duo, McAdoo in effect took a walk, endorsing the ticket so feebly that Davis considered it treachery. Four years later McAdoo would endorse Al Smith in comparable fashion.

Had McAdoo won the nomination during the 1920s, he would likely have had no chance whatsoever of election to the presidency. True, for all of his warts, he remained the leading Democratic Progressive of the decade. It was, however, not a Progressive decade. With the Progressive movement disintegrating, McAdoo found himself confined to the role that other Democrats before and since have played—men such as William Jennings Bryan, Adlai Stevenson, or Hubert Humphrey. Each man arrived at the right place with good ideas, but at the wrong time. The Democratic Party has proved remarkably fecund in producing such presidential candidates, many of them never nominated—Estes Kefauver, for example, or Edmund Muskie. The simple fact is that *no* Democrat was electable to the presidency during the 1920s.

In my book *Reform and Reaction in Twentieth Century American Politics*, I have implicitly attempted to explain this hopeless-candidacy syndrome by exploring conditions that typify the demise of reform movements such as Progressivism, the New Deal, and the Kennedy-Johnson 1960s. What can people expect as these movements die? First, the importance of the crises that precipitated reform to begin with—such as anxiety over corporate abuse of the public, fear of class upheaval, or worries about equal rights—will dissipate in the public mind. Distracting, polarizing ethno-cultural-religious issues move to the fore, which occurred during the 1920s clash pitting the rural South and West against the urban Northeast, Protestants against Catholics, and the countryside against the cities. These cultural splits can turn reform veterans into parodies of themselves by distracting them from matters of economics and class and toward such issues as religion. The first name that comes to mind is William Jennings Bryan around 1924 and 1925. The Scopes trial made Bryan a virtual cartoon of the earlier man. McAdoo, as his legatee, suffered a similar fate over the Klan issue.

Second, when reform eras end, a falloff occurs in purpose and focus among reformers themselves. Often they drop out of politics. Sometimes they die. Not even one of the five or six great leaders of Progressivism, for example, survived into the 1930s. Popular attitudes change, and idealism subsides. Materialism mounts. The 1920s are remembered not so much for public accomplishments as for flappers, bathtub gin, and Al Capone. A general turn from public to private pursuits is noticeable. In literature, the 1920s belonged to George Babbitt and Jay Gatsby.

Third, the prestige of government and the presidency fall as a corresponding rise occurs in the prestige of business and pure moneymaking. Fashions turn away from regulation and providing public services toward laissez-faire, trickle-down economics, and low taxes. Long before Reaganomics, there was Coolidgeomics. McAdoo got caught up in the moneymaking rage of the 1920s. Along with a genuine desire to preserve Wilsonian idealism, McAdoo spoke endlessly and boorishly during these years about his income. In this sense he *was* a statesman grafted onto a promoter.

Fourth, reform-favored groups such as labor lose their cachet as reform eras end. Particularly among intellectuals, rising disillusionment sets in with the mass of the people—with their deservingness of support, their wisdom, even their fundamental rationality. The 1920s was the decade of H. L. Mencken, behaviorism, and Freudianism. Doubt emerged among reformers as to what to pursue next, and their focus and confidence ebbed. They began to seem old-fashioned. Though he had an abundance of confidence, even McAdoo sounded antiquated by 1924. He was trying to build a bridge from Wilsonianism to who knew what? One can say now that he was looking to build a bridge to the New Deal, except that no one in 1920 or 1924 knew that the New Deal was coming. Thus, McAdoo's rhetoric sounded like the wishful afterlife of the Wilson administration and the Progressive movement.

Fifth, as reform ends, the party of reform falls out of favor. A Harding replaces a Wilson in the presidency. The entire period from 1894 through 1928 featured an electoral system dominated by the GOP, with a Democratic resurgence before and during Wilson's presidency. The Democratic Party experienced a disastrous decline following Wilson's second election in 1916. In 1918 it lost its congressional majority. In each election from 1920 through 1926 the Democrats' portion of the national electorate fell. They fared even worse in federal elections than in state and local elections.

Finally, the emergence of a scandal like Teapot Dome further discredits the federal government on which Progressive or liberal reforms depend. Regardless of which party holds power when the scandal erupts, scandals becloud both parties, all politics, and all politicians—particularly if they have ties to someone like E. L. Doheny. "The most amazing thing about the exposure of corruption under President Harding," writes Karl Schriftgiesser in *This was Normalcy: An Account of Party Politics during Twelve Republican Years: 1920-1932* (1948), "is how this was turned, not against the Republican Party, but against those who made the disclosures." Neither Teapot Dome, Watergate, nor Iran-contra proved sufficient in themselves to transform an era of Republican domination into one of Democratic control.

These and many other factors that typify the twilight of reform ended McAdoo's hopes for the presidency, if not the nomination. Had he been the least flawed among Democratic Party Progressives (and he was not), he still would not have stood a chance in the political vortex of the 1920s. He wanted to carry on the Progressive impulse when it was dying, keep to the old course of public purpose while cultural disputes battered his party, and utilize government as its prestige dropped to benefit groups falling out of favor. In 1927 Josephus Daniels, Wilson's secretary of the navy and a McAdoo backer three years before, wrote to FDR: "I believe that [if

McAdoo] had been nominated in 1924 before the bitter feeling of Madison Square [Garden] . . . he would have pulled the labor vote and . . . have won the party many of the dissatisfied farmers in the West, but I do not think he could have been elected." Daniels doubtless read it right.

McAdoo had, as the subtitle of my biography of him suggests, a passion for change, which would certainly have made him a different sort of president from Harding or Coolidge. He displayed astonishing flexibility, but he kept a sensitive finger on the public pulse and rarely let his flexibility or his opportunism carry him giddily beyond it. He lacked any sort of fixed ideological star by which to navigate. His forte involved the use of government to confront many pressing problems at a time. As Ray Stannard Baker put it, "McAdoo has a chain-lightning mind. It not only moves swiftly, but it is not content unless there is quick issue in action. Wilson loved to talk of principles, to make clear the reason for his convictions. McAdoo instantly reduces everything to action. He seems to dislike talking of anything except action—what he did, where he went, what the other people did, and how the whole matter eventuated." Although highly intelligent, McAdoo was not a man of ideas as Wilson was. In this sense he much more resembled Franklin D. Roosevelt.

In 1932, FDR's year, McAdoo dreamed (as Wilson had) of a third crack at the presidency. McAdoo's memoirs, *Crowded Years*, made a timely appearance in 1931. This book stands among the best autobiographies by a 20th-century American political figure. McAdoo remained the heir of Bryan, although McAdoo's southwestern constituency also reflected newer forces, such as big agriculture, railroads, and the oil interests that had earlier gotten him into trouble. When the Speaker of the House of Representatives, John Nance Garner, began accumulating support in California and his native Texas—McAdoo territory—McAdoo decided to back Garner, run for the U.S. Senate, and hope to be drafted as the candidate for president at the Democratic national convention in Chicago. Aided by McAdoo and William Randolph Hearst, Garner took the California primary. By now the most important Democrat in California, McAdoo went to the national convention as head of his state delegation and with every determination of stopping

Roosevelt. By convention time, Roosevelt had a majority of the delegates but fell well short of the two-thirds still required.

As Elliot A. Rosen has written in *Hoover, Roosevelt, and the Brains Trust: From Depression to New Deal* (1977), "The trump cards rested in the hands of the California-Texas group headed by . . . McAdoo and the reticent, hard-drinking poker player, John Nance Garner." Ultimately, the Roosevelt forces realized that they must win over Garner and Hearst. In the end, though, it was McAdoo who "held the key to the convention's outcome." Tortuous negotiations ensued. On the climactic fourth ballot—with everything for FDR on the line—McAdoo stood and approached the platform. A smile lighted up his features. He declared: "California came here to nominate a President of the United States. She did not come here to deadlock this convention or to engage in another disastrous contest like that of 1924. . . . California casts forty-four votes for Franklin D. Roosevelt." There was an uproar. Al Smith's supporters raged from the galleries as in 1924. McAdoo thanked them for "the compliment." "Good old McAdoo!" Roosevelt exclaimed. Minutes later, FDR was nominated. McAdoo returned to California with three guarantees: control of the state's patronage, veto power over the Cabinet choices for State and Treasury, and Garner as the pick for vice president.

His senatorial campaign a success, McAdoo voted down the line for the New Deal and backed FDR in the Supreme Court fight. With his optimism, his boyish enthusiasm, his unphilosophical bent toward problem-solving, and his great flexibility, he had really been a temperamental New Dealer all along. Indeed, he belongs to a tradition that began with Bryan in 1896 and climaxed with FDR in 1936: the attempt to build a coalition of workers and farmers that would ensure Democratic Party hegemony. Wilson briefly forged such a coalition in 1916, but Roosevelt created the definitive version 20 years later. The oil scandal, Klan, and prohibition issues undermined McAdoo's own attempt.

If some of McAdoo's shortcomings were personal and idiosyncratic (the pronounced power-driven opportunism and the desire for money), others were products of his time, an era ostensibly dry and indifferent or hostile to civil rights. Ultimately, McAdoo was unique among figures of equivalent stature in the early 1900s: a former businessman who instructed management about its obligations to labor but could work with both groups; a male feminist; a rural figurehead who was an urbanite; and above all, a governmentalist. One sees in him a bit of each of the genuinely great Progressives—Theodore Roosevelt, Bryan, Wilson, and La Follette. Though utterly doomed as a presidential candidate, McAdoo ranks among the few major Progressives who made a happy transition to the New Deal version of the welfare state. As an aside I might add that, like FDR, McAdoo played his cards close to his vest and at important points can seem maddeningly difficult to comprehend.

McAdoo's story has one final twist. Defeated in the 1938 California primary, he went on to become a president after all—the president of the board of American President shipping lines. He died in 1941.

QUESTION: Did anyone ever question the legitimacy of the Ku Klux Klan? It was officially dissolved by the Grand Wizard after the Civil War.

MR. BROESAMLE: It was then reborn, unfortunately, in 1915. In fact, this issue is one of considerable sensitivity to me right now. The students on the campus where I teach have just invited the most notorious Klansman of recent years, David Duke, to speak on a much-debated affirmative action proposition pending on California's ballot. Evidently, the controversial influence of the KKK resonates as much now as it did in McAdoo's time. The Klan was reorganized by a group of people that included a gifted salesman named Edward Y. Clarke. By the mid-1920s, it had over four million members, and its popularity had increased greatly. Its glory years in the 20th century were from 1920 to 1925. In the 1920s a large group of Klansmen paraded through the streets of Washington, D.C. The Klan controlled a considerable number of states, including possibly California. The governor of California, Friend Richardson, may have been a secret member. In states such as Alabama (where Hugo Black was a member) or Missouri (Harry Truman), it really paid to belong. Interestingly, the Klan also had a powerful women's auxiliary. These women could be notorious, mounting whispering campaigns in their small towns against

Catholic or Jewish merchants. In an odd way, they were also proto-feminists in the sense that they demanded an independent Klan voice for themselves. They even wore their own white bedsheets.

Once the Klan had taken political power, it did not know what to do with that power. It was a protest organization, and in power it could not develop an effective program. Much like the Socialist Party of the United States in the early 20th century, it existed to mount one protracted scream. One of the things about the second Klan that differentiates it from the first Klan is that it reached its apogee of power not in the South, but in the Midwest. The most powerful states under Klan control were Ohio and Indiana. This new Klan was mainly a midwestern and western organization, very powerful in Orange County and Riverside County in California, for example. It also had a good deal of power in the cities, even though two-thirds of the Klan members lived in domains of less than 100,000. It thus differed in important ways from the original Klan. It was more ultranationalist, xenophobic, antiforeign, anti-Catholic, and anti-Semitic. The fact that it was anti-black was almost a secondary consideration.

By 1924 or 1925, the Klan came to grief, and by 1925 it was on a second precipitous slide as a consequence of the notorious Stephenson rape case in Indiana. This case involved another aspect of the Klan. The Klan sought out fallen characters in its small town and rural domains, particularly fallen women, whom it would strip naked and beat. It claimed to stand for the old moralities, yet its standing for the old moralities took these kinds of perverse forms. The head of the Indiana Klan was a nationally famous multimillionaire named Stephenson, who sexually assaulted a state employee named Madge Oberholtzer. She took poison, and he went to the penitentiary. That event was like the popping of a balloon. By 1925, the Klan was already under attack in important states, and this incident finished it. It was reborn in prominence in the 1940s and 1950s in reaction to the civil rights movement, but it never achieved the status and importance it had in the 1920s.

The 1924 convention and the battle over the Klan within the Democratic Party occurred at a point when the Klan was at its apogee. Did McAdoo love the Klan? Did Al Smith want to take on the Klan? No, Smith did not want this naming battle. Another important voice inside the New York delegation who warned the delegation to avoid conflict over the Klan was FDR. In the end, however, this issue was a useful wedge to break McAdoo's candidacy. McAdoo had no end of advice from those around him, including his own campaign manager, to denounce the Klan, and he simply would not do it. Wilson's assistant secretary of state, Breckinridge Long, reminded him that the Klan was a core of his support and that he did not dare assume an anti-Klan posture. McAdoo agreed, and he stuck by that decision, much to his detriment.

COMMENT: I would have thought that the new Klan would have made a point of distinguishing itself from the old Klan.

MR. BROESAMLE: I suspect that they got tremendous mileage from their claim that they were continuing the spirit of the old organization. It is not a coincidence that the movie *Birth of a Nation*, which glorified the Klan, was made in 1915, the same time as the neo-bedsheet craze. In fact, all of the current arguments about family values and cultural defeat, a reaction to the 1960s, are reminiscent of the cultural struggles of the 1920s. The symbolism that hovers around Bill Clinton is evocative of the symbolism that hovered around people as diverse as McAdoo or Al Smith. These people encountered moral and cultural dilemmas that served as wedges to thwart reform intentions, often successfully.

For example, Bill Clinton had a number of intentions reminiscent of the New Deal era or of the Great Society. The health care reform plan is a key example. Those plans have essentially been shattered. The 1994 congressional elections were devastating. Will Clinton achieve anything as extensive as what Lyndon Johnson or John Kennedy had in mind? The big question is whether he will turn left or cleave to the middle throughout his second term. Reform presidents typically go left in their second terms. FDR, Woodrow Wilson, and the Kennedy-Johnson team are good examples of this trend.

John J. Broesamle

COMMENT: When you discussed Progressivism, you did not mention the Progressive Party, which actually emerged at that time. La Follette carried Wisconsin in the 1924 election.

MR. BROESAMLE: He did take some electoral votes. I compiled some voting percentages of the presidential campaigns from 1924 to 1929. In 1924, Calvin Coolidge received 382 electoral votes, and Davis, the final Democratic candidate, received 136. Bob La Follette, however, received one-sixth of the popular vote, which was similar to Perot receiving 19 percent of the vote in 1992.

In the 1924 presidential election, many votes that would have gone to McAdoo shifted to La Follette after the Teapot Dome incident and the revelations about McAdoo. When Davis was nominated, McAdoo did everything he could to keep his distance from that campaign. Davis considered McAdoo's rejection of him as treachery. Finally, McAdoo did grudgingly endorse Davis at the eleventh hour in an endorsement that sounded much more like one for Bob La Follette. In essence he said that La Follette was the best candidate but could not possibly win because he ran on a third-party ticket, so unfortunately, the better choice was Davis. Davis considered McAdoo a traitor for another reason as well. After the revelations about Doheny, many of the railway unions that supported McAdoo changed their support to La Follette. La Follette called for complete railroad nationalization on a permanent basis and conservation of natural resources, which were two of his key issues.

La Follette was like so many other leading Progressives—by 1925 or 1926, they were gone. If La Follette, Theodore Roosevelt, Wilson, Bryan, or Socialist leader Eugene Debs had lived longer, circumstances could have been very different.

QUESTION: You said that McAdoo delivered 44 votes for California and put Roosevelt over the top in 1932. Did McAdoo receive some privileges for that support?

MR. BROESAMLE: McAdoo wanted to be drafted for the nomination, but he decided that, pending a draft, he would run for the Senate in California. By the time of the Democratic National

21

Convention in Chicago, McAdoo was the most powerful Democrat in California. Incidentally, McAdoo, who had a fierce temper, was furious at Roosevelt's handlers for accepting the support and backing of an anti-McAdoo faction in the San Francisco Bay area that was headed by conservative former supporters of Al Smith. McAdoo entered the convention determined to block Roosevelt, but he was ultimately persuaded to change his mind. The key voice in this persuasion was Daniel Roper, who had been a McAdoo manager in the 1920s and who later became Roosevelt's commerce secretary. Roper reminded McAdoo that if Roosevelt were not nominated, a conservative would be. A viable prospect was Newton Baker of Ohio, who stood far to the right on domestic issues. McAdoo had no use at all for Baker. McAdoo realized that if he broke Roosevelt's candidacy, he would be responsible for the nomination of a conservative to the Democratic candidacy.

Apparently, the California delegation as a whole wanted to remain with Garner for one more ballot. Roosevelt's handlers were convinced that unless Roosevelt could win a majority on the fourth ballot, Baker would be the nominee. It was absolutely critical to win California. If California went, it would start a bandwagon effect on that ballot, which it did. McAdoo was willing to trust Roosevelt to preserve Progressivism in the party, but in return, McAdoo wanted certain things. In exchange for convincing his delegation to support Roosevelt on the fourth ballot, McAdoo wanted control of the state's patronage for obvious reasons—he wanted the San Francisco Bay group neutered. He was also given veto power over the nominations for the secretaries of treasury and state. The individuals nominated were William H. Woodin and Cordell Hull, who were both acceptable to McAdoo and Roosevelt, so there was no problem in this area. Garner, the man whom McAdoo had backed, was the vice-presidential nominee. Roper became secretary of commerce.

The entire arrangement is still quite murky. Smith supporters had thought that they had a deal with McAdoo in which they would go every round against Roosevelt. Smith was bitterly jealous of Roosevelt and thus even more powerfully disposed to defeat Roosevelt. He and his supporters cried treachery to the end, thinking that McAdoo had betrayed them. McAdoo changed his mind because they would not name their presidential candidate choice. McAdoo returned to his delegation, and they agreed that a small breakout group would work and speak for the delegation. Finally, at the eleventh hour, the small group decided that they would vote for Roosevelt on the fourth ballot. The galleries were furious. McAdoo thoroughly enjoyed the melee and was avenged for what they had done to him in 1924. McAdoo did not come away empty-handed, and in return, he was an absolutely loyal New Deal supporter.

QUESTION: Did McAdoo abandon his earlier values at that time, or did he achieve his goals through his support of Roosevelt?

MR. BROESAMLE: It is difficult to expose the inner core of this man. He was an opportunist. Unlike Wilson, however, he did not revel in thinking through the reasons for his actions. He was a distinctive pragmatist and had an aggressive businessman's mind. Some of his business calculations were disastrous, yet by 1908 he was running the largest subaqueous tunnel system in the world under the Hudson River as well as the largest office complex on earth, located where the World Trade Center now stands.

I have become convinced that McAdoo's ultimate sentiment was governmentalist; in other words, without being a socialist, he believed that government was far from doing everything it needed to do on behalf of the interests that concerned him, such as shipping and railroads. He wanted a five-year plan in which the government would continue to run rail lines into the 1920s or possibly nationalize the rail lines. When Bryan said similar things, he was accused of being a socialist. McAdoo continued in the same tone in the 1920s, but Congress would not hear of it. Consequently, railroads reverted to private control in March 1920. McAdoo was the sort of person that the business community never trusted, and for good reason, since he was an instinctive governmentalist.

McAdoo was very comfortable with the most liberal aspects of Wilsonian reform. For example, he supported taxes to the highest-ever rate of 63 percent during World War I and the redistribution of funds through taxation during the 1920s. He supported the New Deal right through the Supreme Court fight, which drove many

Democrats away, particularly Southern Democrats. When the Court packing plan was read, Garner stood in the back of the Senate chamber holding his nose with one hand and shaking a down-turned thumb with the other. McAdoo was perfectly compatible with the New Deal because he did not believe in restricting governmental power. His general rule of thumb was that more government was better. If Roosevelt was for more government, that goal was fine with McAdoo. McAdoo was the proponent of New Deal ideas in the 1920s at a time when it was unfashionable to do so.

Otis L. Graham Jr. wrote an important book entitled *An Encore for Reform: The Old Progressives and the New Deal* (1967) on the transition of old Progressives into the New Deal and found that most did not support it. McAdoo, on the other hand, was a striking exception.

QUESTION: Were there any indicators of this inclination in his early background?

MR. BROESAMLE: McAdoo was a Cleveland Democrat as a young man and opposed William Jennings Bryan—something Bryan remembered in later years when they fought together to get Wilson a nomination in 1912. McAdoo did what many Progressives did. Public attitudes were different at different times throughout the Progressive Era—the first 15 years of this century. Progressivism itself changed, as did individuals. Bryan, Theodore Roosevelt, and McAdoo were all different men in 1915 than they were in 1905. McAdoo was in favor of sound money, but he was never a businessman representative of the Gilded Age in the early 20th century, nor was he ever regarded that way. He never hid the fact that he was highly suspicious of Wall Street. McAdoo's company became famous for its public relations policy—what he called the public-be-pleased policy. He paid his labor well and treated them fairly. Those tunnels were constructed under the Hudson under McAdoo's direction in a vastly more efficient manner than the efficiency in which the Los Angeles subway system is being built today. He charged fair tolls and took public suggestions. This approach may sound like welfare capitalism or like a ploy, but McAdoo was sincere in his approach. He spoke openly for women's rights and the rights of Jews to travel freely in Russia.

McAdoo had a sunny side, which was evident in his business career. He was first a promoter in the private sector and then a few years later a promoter of bigger government in the public sector, but he was always a promoter. Lippmann was right to say that McAdoo was a statesman grafted onto a promoter—not fully fair, but completely correct. The promoter came first, and the governmentalist conjoined.

McAdoo was after power, money, and recognition, but he was also after good causes. Very few men were outspoken feminists in those years. He gave his feminist beliefs practical applications. Women working in ticket booths in the Hudson and Manhattan Railway system, which he founded, were paid the same as male ticket-sellers. Later in the public sector, he provided equal pay for men and women when he ran the nation's railroad network. McAdoo was a promoter, a governmentalist, and an opportunist.

NARRATOR: Thank you for adding an illuminating part to the Miller Center's continuing discussion of prominent statesmen who never became president but were nonetheless important and noteworthy figures in American politics.

CHAPTER TWO

James G. Blaine*

DAVID F. HEALY

NARRATOR: Professor David Healy of the University of Wisconsin in Milwaukee completed his bachelor's, master's, and doctoral degrees in U.S. history at the University of Wisconsin-Madison, with a Ph.D. minor in Latin American history. He taught at Illinois College (1960-64), the University of Delaware (1964-66), and at the University of Wisconsin-Milwaukee (1966-1993), where he is currently Professor Emeritus.

Professor Healy has published books and articles on imperialism, U.S.-Latin American relations, and late 19th-century U.S. history. His subject today is James G. Blaine, a man who has been viewed with some misgivings by reformers, but who nevertheless deserves a place in our series on statesmen who were never president.

MR. HEALY: James G. Blaine is a man on whom there is little consensus but who is impossible to ignore. A leading American political figure of the Gilded Age, James G. Blaine was a potential presidential nominee through five Republican nominating conventions and the Republican presidential candidate in 1884, an election

---

Presented in a Forum at the Miller Center of Public Affairs on 23 February 1996.

that he narrowly lost. He was also a major shaper of the modern Republican Party, a distinguished Speaker of the House of Representatives, and twice secretary of state, the position for which historians best remember him. With a large, passionately loyal following in the Republican Party and an only slightly smaller body of people inside and outside of the party who desperately hated him, Blaine was always at the center of controversy and the subject of strong emotion. Andrew Dixon White, diplomat and educator, once said, "Mr. Blaine was certainly the most fascinating man I have ever known in politics. No wonder that so many Republicans in all parts of the country seem ready to give their lives to elect him." Senator George F. Hoar, a Republican of Massachusetts, expressed a slightly different opinion: "There has probably never been a man in our history upon whom so few people looked with indifference. He was born to be loved or hated. Nobody occupied a middle ground as to him."

James Blaine was brilliant, charismatic, energetic, and bold, but despite being such a uniquely memorable figure, he was largely forgotten a generation after he died. Moreover, 20th-century textbook writers and historians have tended to portray him as an archetype of Gilded Age corruption, so he is remembered largely in a way that validates the principal charges of his enemies. Such views, however, are often arbitrary and reflect only a partial reading of Blaine's record. Interest in James Blaine has experienced an upsurge lately, and among the last generation of historiographers, Blaine's historical reputation has considerably improved. In almost every field, improvements in how his record is interpreted is taking place.

James Blaine was born in 1830 in Pennsylvania. At age 13, he went to Washington and Jefferson College at a time when few people went to college. After graduation, he taught school for six years in Kentucky and Philadelphia. His political career would not begin until 1853 when he moved to Augusta, Maine, where his wife's relatives lived. There, he became the editor of *Kennebec Journal,* a leading local Whig organ at a time when the Whig Party was in the process of disintegrating. Blaine then joined the Republican Party as it was being born, and he rose with the Republicans in Maine and, soon, the nation.

David F. Healy

After serving in the state legislature, Blaine went to the House of Representatives in 1863 as a Lincoln Republican at a time when there were few Lincoln Republicans in Congress. Once Blaine got to the House of Representatives, he experienced a meteoric rise. He was recognized almost at once as a brilliant and talented newcomer with a future before him, which proved to be true. Only six years after entering the House, Blaine became Speaker, a position that he would hold for another six years until the Democrats obtained a majority in 1875. Blaine is remembered as a distinguished Speaker and as a particularly able man with the strength of character necessary to handle an unruly House. He had total knowledge of parliamentary maneuvering, and for once he managed to restrain his partisanship so that he had a good reputation on both sides of the aisle. This would be the last time, however.

By 1876 Blaine had emerged as the bright young man of the party, the glittering man of the future, and the front-runner for the presidential nomination of the Republican Party. The better-organized forces of the old-timers, however, beat him and ultimately chose Rutherford B. Hayes. Following that loss, Blaine went to the Senate, where he was appointed to a Maine vacancy that he could occupy indefinitely. He tried for the nomination again in 1880 when Ulysses Grant was trying to re-acquire the presidency from Hayes for a third term. A body of partisans in the Republican Party had wanted Grant back in power because Hayes had been difficult about patronage appointments and Grant had always been very good about them. Consequently, Grant had a strong backing for the nomination. The only comparable competitor was Blaine, whose loyal following was big enough to deadlock the convention. Neither side would give way, however. Neither camp saw many defections, and after 30-odd ballots, it was clearly time to look for a third choice. From the several people being considered, Blaine threw his weight behind James A. Garfield, an old friend and House colleague who then was nominated and elected. In the brief Garfield administration, Blaine became the leading figure not only as secretary of state but as a kind of prime minister and principal eminence. After four months, however, Garfield was shot and then

29

died two months later, which means that Blaine's glory was short-lived.

Vice President Chester Arthur consequently became president after Garfield's death. Because Arthur and Blaine were not close and came from different wings of the party, Blaine resigned after less than a year in the Cabinet and waited for his turn in 1884. This time he did get the nomination, but he lost by a whisker to Grover Cleveland in one of those typically close elections of the day.

Four years later in the 1888 election, Blaine took himself out of contention, looked over the field, and threw his weight behind Benjamin Harrison. Once again, Blaine's support was sufficient to make Harrison the nominee, and again Blaine was repaid with the position of secretary of state. He served in that position for three years before resigning in the summer of 1892. Blaine died in January 1893.

In domestic politics, Blaine's role is remembered in history as one of a small group of leaders in the Republican Party who reshaped it after the Civil War and Reconstruction. This group defined new issues that the Republican Party would support and put the party into new harmony with the times. While the Democratic Party continued to be a loose coalition of city machines and southern states, the Republican Party in the 1880s gradually took on a focus and a direction that made it a national party. With the aid of others, Blaine repositioned the Republicans as a party of industrialization and economic growth. They favored protective tariffs for industry and sound money for investors. They opposed inflation in all forms, including greenbackers and free silver rights, which is one reason some farmers did not like Blaine. Blaine and other Republicans also supported railroad subsidies. Less successfully, Blaine tried to get subsidies for the merchant marine and other special groups. He always supported government policies that were favorable to business, and he helped to make the Republican Party the party of business, particularly large enterprise and big business. He had close ties to all of the top business leaders of his day, particularly Andrew Carnegie, financier Stephen B. Elkins of West Virginia, and W. W. Phelps, who inherited a huge New Jersey fortune. One of his sons married the daughter of Cyrus McCormick, the farm machinery tycoon. He was very close to these people.

In foreign policy Blaine focused on Latin America. He wanted U.S. leadership in that region. He wanted to keep Latin America stabilized and at peace in order to nurture trade and particularly to block British political influence and trade competition. None of these things were particularly original to Blaine, but he was ready to move more vigorously and to take more of the powers of government in tow.

Blaine envisioned large institutional arrangements like hemispheric customs unions and the Pan American Union. In fact, Blaine presided over the first Pan American Conference. Even though he was a protectionist, he pushed for reciprocal trade agreements because Latin American products were not competitive with those of the United States. Blaine was also eager to build a canal across Central America, and he tried to get the British to change their canal treaty so that neither country would have sole control of it. He failed, however, to persuade the British to accept major modifications in the Clayton-Bulwer Treaty.

Blaine had a rather definite, large, and ambitious agenda. He was skillful and effective in domestic politics, but much less so in foreign policy. During his first term as secretary of state under Garfield and Arthur, Blaine was inexperienced and overambitious. He tried to do far too much in too little time. He also overestimated American influence and was weakened by an inept foreign service and amateur diplomats abroad. He tried diplomatic intervention in the War of the Pacific in which Peru and Bolivia fought Chile, intervening after the Chileans won a decisive military victory. He tried to prevent them from annexing territory, but having paid for it largely in blood, the Chileans were absolutely determined to proceed with annexation. Blaine's efforts to jawbone or bluff the Chileans out of territory turned out to be a total fiasco.

As secretary of state under Harrison, Blaine was older, wiser, more experienced, more moderate, and more realistic. He narrowed his focus and worked more effectively toward his goals, as exemplified by the Pan American Conference and the reciprocity treaties that he successfully passed through Congress but which died shortly thereafter.

Increasingly, however, Blaine was hampered by bad health. Around the time that he became Harrison's secretary of state,

Blaine's health began to fail, and he became increasingly ill. As his absences increased, he began to lose his grip on policy, and others began to move in. A secretary of state must constantly be alert because so many people want a part of policy. Finally, Blaine resigned and soon after died.

Despite his accomplishments, Blaine is very persistently seen only in terms of his quest for the presidency. Only Henry Clay was a viable presidential prospect for as long as Blaine was. Blaine's enemies, who were numerous and bitter, pictured him as always plotting for the presidency and saw everything he did as another ploy, another maneuver, to get to the White House. Such a portrayal is quite clearly an exaggeration. Certainly Blaine wanted to be president. This was evident in a 1879 letter he wrote to his loyal supporter, the editor of the *New York Tribune*, about the upcoming 1880 campaign:

> If the great American people don't choose to nominate me for the presidency, as they almost certainly will not, they will not find me a fool or a weakling or a sorehead or a mourner. But I shall go into the campaign of 1880 for the candidate with all the cheerfulness in the world. I enjoy my place in the Senate, and unless the deuce comes to be counted as the ace in Maine, I can hold it indefinitely. Why, then, should I have to get into a doubtful contest? Had I succeeded in 1876, I would now be on the eve of mustering out at 50 years of age.

He goes on to say that all past presidents had found misery in the office, but he ended by saying, "Therefore, with all these warnings before me like the English lady's horror of the bullfight and her eager desire to see one, it only remains for me to say that of course I would enjoy being made miserable after the pattern of these illustrious predecessors, but heavens, what a letter I am writing and with what reckless candor I am talking!" Blaine wanted to be president. There was no question about it, and everyone knew it. He just never achieved that goal.

Aside from the usual circumstances, conditions, happenstances, and accidents, three main barriers stood in the way of his presidency: charges of corruption, enemies within the Republican Party, and bad health.

Corruption charges were first launched only two weeks before the 1876 Republican National Convention. The charges originated not from the Democrats, but from another faction of the Republicans who supported Benjamin Bristow, a weaker candidate for the nomination, and hoped to cripple the front-runner to help their man. The Democrats soon took up the cry, however, and from that time until practically the end of his career, Blaine was barraged by an endless stream of accusations of every kind of corruption—some of them fantastic, many of them unlikely, some of them probable, but virtually all of them unproven. The charges were much more numerous than a busy man could have achieved in a long life.

The most enduring charge concerns Blaine's connection to the Little Rock and Fort Smith Railroad Company and the Union Pacific Railroad Company. In a tangle of accusations that kept multiplying, Blaine was variously accused of receiving $75,000 from Union Pacific president, Thomas Scott, for the almost worthless Little Rock bonds; profiting from brokering the bonds to buyers in an insider deal and then seeing them lose their money; and other variations on the theme. Blaine quite convincingly rebutted these claims and seemed to have cleared himself when James Mulligan showed up in Washington with a bundle of letters.

James Mulligan had been a clerk for Blaine's brother who had fired him, possibly providing the animus for Mulligan's charges against Blaine. Later, Mulligan worked for a business associate of Blaine's in Boston, with whom Blaine had had a number of dealings. Having control of the files, Mulligan took a number of letters written by Blaine that Mulligan alleged proved Blaine's corruption. He announced this loudly in advance so everyone would eagerly await the specifics. When he arrived in Washington, Blaine went to his hotel room and asked to see the letters. Mulligan gave him the letters but exacted a promise from Blaine for their return. Blaine did this several times, each time handing the letters back until Mulligan forgot to get the promise, at which point Blaine put them in his pocket and departed, saying they were his personal property and no one else had a right to them.

With these letters in hand, Blaine went to the floor of the House of Representatives and passionately defended his total innocence. He told everyone that he would read to them the portions of the letters that were relevant to the charges. He then read what he chose to read. His supporters said he cleared himself triumphantly. His critics, of course, said he had done no such thing and had never shown the letters. He refused ever to let the letters become public. Ultimately, Blaine chose two prominent lawyers, one from each party, to read the letters. After reading them, these lawyers wrote and signed a document stating that they did not support the charges against Blaine. That effort still did not end the matter, however, and from then on the Mulligan letters would dog Blaine until his death.

The attention paid to this controversy has endured beyond Blaine's death. It is included in many textbooks and college history lectures that cover the politicking of the Gilded Age. There is no question that Blaine profited from inside tips from big business friends. He was included in deals and clearly benefited from his influence and his considerable connections. He borrowed $30,000 from Jay Cooke, for example, to help build a mansion in Washington, D.C.—money that Cooke was afraid to refuse because of Blaine's influence. Blaine was helpful to big business and very specific about some of the ways they were helpful to him in return when he made a good deal of money—ways that would be considered ethically questionable, though not unusual. Blaine's activities were never proven to be illegal, yet some of the charges against him are probably true.

Being the most colorful and leading figure in the Republican Party, Blaine was also the target of the most abuse from both jealous rivals within the party and from the Democrats. Reformers and good government people, in particular, saw him as having horns and hooves. On top of that, Blaine strongly opposed civil service reform, as did most politicians of the day, because political patronage appointments were the glue that held the machinery together. Followers were rewarded with appointments and jobs. Without those, it was felt that a viable party organization was not possible and the whole system would fall apart. Among public reformers like E. L. Godkin of the *Nation* and the *New York Evening*

Post, Blaine's double crime of being tied to corruption and opposing civil service reform made him an object of absolute obsession.

These corruption charges on the whole did not move many votes, but they did have an effect. Blaine supporters claimed it was all partisanship and slander by political enemies and that his critics did not like him whether he was innocent or guilty. They probably did not move many votes, but they were a marginal factor in a very close election. Anything marginal can be vital. Hence, these charges did have something to do with his ultimate failure to gain the presidency. Every negative factor is one more hurdle to overcome.

The second barrier in the way of Blaine's presidency was the split of the Republican Party into two factions in the 1880s—the so-called stalwarts, who were supporters of General Grant and his administration and later of his renomination, and their opponents, called the "half-breeds." Blaine became the leading half-breed by blocking Grant's nomination in 1880. The stalwarts never forgave him because it was Grant's last chance.

Several of these stalwart leaders also ran large state Republican organizations. The most important of them probably was Roscoe Conkling, who headed the New York State Republican organization and also happened to be Blaine's bitterest personal enemy. This situation goes back to a quarrel they had in the House of Representatives in 1865. The following excerpt will provide some flavor of Gilded Age rhetoric:

> Conkling and Blaine, in fact, had been deadly adversaries ever since a debate in the lower house in April 1865 over a matter of patronage connected with the provost marshal's department. Conkling had attacked the officer in question, and Blaine had upheld him, taking the occasion also to twit Conkling for alleged irregularities during the war. Then in his domineering manner, a very mountain of conceit and pride, all swelling with anger, the member from New York had said among other cruel things. . .
> "If I have fallen to the necessity of taking lessons from that gentleman, God help me. If the gentleman from Maine had the least idea of how profoundly indifferent I am to his opinion on the subject which he has been discussing or upon any other

subject personal to me, I think he would hardly take the trouble to rise here and express his opinion.

Conkling was a master of invective, an imperious man with enormous pride who often silenced people with their own fear of the hammer blows of his rhetoric.

To Conkling's remarks, however, Blaine replied with neither anger nor fear but with pure mockery, "The contempt of that large-minded gentleman is so wilting. His haughty disdain, his grand eloquent swell, his majestic super-eminent, overpowering, turkey-gobbler strut has been so crushing to myself and to all the men of this House that I know it was the act of the greatest temerity for me to venture upon a controversy with him." After Blaine's comments, the congressmen began to laugh. Moreover, the "turkey-gobbler strut" phrase clung to Conkling, and he never forgave Blaine. From that time on, they were enemies. In 1884 when Blaine ran for president, Conkling had retired from public life and was practicing law in New York. When they asked him if he would support the Blaine campaign, he simply said, "I don't take criminal cases."

The third barrier standing in Blaine's way was bad health. Blaine was a man of enormous energy, but he was also a hypochondriac. When his batteries ran down, he would take to his bed and persuade himself that he was sick and wait until his energy returned. Consequently, it took a while for his friends to realize that in later life he became very sick indeed. He contracted Bright's disease, a kidney ailment that weakened him progressively beginning in 1887 and finally led to his death at age 63. After 1884 and in the succeeding campaigns, he was not in good enough health to attempt the presidency.

He refused to be considered for the nomination in 1888 when, according to general consensus, he could have had the nomination for the asking and would have won the election. He said that defeated candidates had no right to seek a second chance; that only if there was a sort of unanimous request by acclamation should they accept a nomination, something that would never happen due to a factionalized party. Although he probably meant that when he said it, whether he would have felt so strongly about it had he been in good health might be questionable. As his health began to fail,

Blaine confided to his intimates that he thought the stresses of another presidential run might kill him.

By 1892 Blaine was a dying man with only a few months left to live. Even so, he was put in contention for the nomination against Harrison, who wanted to be renominated himself. Blaine took himself out again and declared he was not a candidate. Oddly enough, he was put into the race by a clutch of stalwart bosses who were furious at Harrison for blocking patronage appointments and hoped to get rid of him. They knew that only Blaine was a potent enough force to do so, but by then, most people realized that Blaine's time had passed. Blaine did come in a long second of the two contenders, but he was not really running in 1892 and had no real chance of winning.

In short, James Blaine was a major figure in five nominating conventions. He was responsible for choosing the nominee in three conventions: in 1880 when he threw his weight to Garfield, in 1884 when he achieved it himself, and in 1888 when he successfully supported Harrison. An examination of the presidential election of 1884, therefore, ought to improve our understanding of why James Blaine never became president.

Presidential elections in the 1880s were incredibly close. In 1880, Garfield had a popular majority of 0.1 percent. In 1884, Blaine lost by 0.2 percent of the popular vote, and Harrison won in 1888 by 0.9 percent of the popular vote. Because elections were balanced on a knife edge, little room was left in which to maneuver. The whole solid South was Democratic; the old Confederacy had voted Democratic in all national elections for decades. Much of the northeast normally voted Republican. The Midwest had a few swing states, but they were not dependable either way and tended to balance out. The crucial state was New York, a genuine swing state that was by far the weightiest in terms of electoral votes. New York City tended to be dominated by the Tammany Democratic machine. Upstate was dominated by Republicans. Typically in this period, New York determined who won the election.

In 1881 an economic recession hurt the Republicans since the administration was Republican at that time. In off-year elections in 1882, the Democrats took away 72 seats in the House, which at that time was a very large number of seats. The momentum worked in favor of the Democrats, and Blaine's nomination at the Chicago convention was sold basically on the basis that only Blaine, as their strongest and most popular candidate, had a chance of winning in 1884.

Blaine's nomination did meet opposition, however. Chester Arthur had wanted to be renominated and held the Southern patronage and therefore the delegates from the South, but Arthur was not a strong figure and was easily brushed aside by the Blaine forces. Consequently, Blaine's nomination made at least two groups unhappy. First, there were the stalwarts, who were still rather solidly against Blaine at this time. This opposition had additional ramifications because Roscoe Conkling was still very much the leader of his part of New York, despite being out of politics. Also, Chester Arthur, the incumbent president and a stalwart leader, was angry at Blaine. Arthur refused to support Blaine or do anything to help him in the campaign. New York was thus going to be harder than usual for a Republican to carry because he would not have the usual Republican support there.

Second, Blaine's nomination alienated the reformers and the good government people led by Carl Schurz, E. L. Godkin, George William Curtis of *Harper's Weekly*, and others. This small group of elite Easterners all tended to have connections or control of large publications. As a result, both Democrats and Independent Republicans in New York City called on everyone to desert Blaine and vote for Grover Cleveland, presumably the good government man and the new Democratic find from Buffalo. Only two major New York newspapers supported Blaine: the *New York Tribune*, which was edited by his close friend, and the *Commercial Advertiser*. Aside from the weight of the reformist group themselves, the press had shifted a bit sideways by this publicity.

Incidentally, the Independent Republicans were the target of enormous abuse and jeering from the regular Republicans, who labeled them "mugwumps." The name has stuck—ever since they have been known not as Independent Republicans but as mugwumps. Mugwumps are the people who split from Blaine in 1884. The 1884 election was perhaps the nastiest election in American history. It was dominated by mud-slinging on both sides. The Buffalo Republican clique, for example, circulated all kinds of stories about Cleveland's depravity, which upon investigation proved to be totally false. Meanwhile, the Democrats went into a frenzy of charges of corruption, adding some new charges to the old ones. Some of the Democrats fabricated stories about Blaine's private life and various unfaithful actions that were equally baseless. Blaine and his wife were a devoted couple, had a close marriage, loved their children, and had an ideal family. As one Democratic wit essentially said, "Since Blaine is such an adornment to private life and Cleveland to public, let's leave one in private life and put the other one in the White House." There was not that much difference in the programs or the platforms in 1884, although everyone knew that Blaine stood for protectionism and business advantage.

In the 1884 election, Blaine also had to deal with James Mulligan again. Mulligan had resurfaced in the heat of the campaign with a new batch of letters, which he published this time. The letters were inconclusive, but distinctly compromising. On the worst of them, Blaine had written "Burn this letter." Instead of burning it, however, the recipient filed it in the normal way. As a result, Mulligan was later able to find it. After the letters were made public, crowds marched through the streets in hordes chanting "James G. Blaine, the continental liar from the state of Maine. Burn this letter." In one parade the Democrats turned out 40,000 people in New York City. They had enormous rallies in those days, and these chants with drums and bands gave it great élan.

The Republicans acted in much the same fashion. The situation regarding the Mulligan letters worried Republicans until enemies of Grover Cleveland suddenly revealed that he had fathered an illegitimate child. In the Victorian Age, such information could be pretty damaging, and the Democrats were in total panic. They were rushing around trying to figure out how to cover it up when Cleveland, who never wanted for guts, said, "Tell the truth." For the Democrats, this would be their salvation. If they had tried to cover it up, they would have been lost. Cleveland publicly announced that he had fathered this child and had supported it, and that the public could do what it wished with the knowledge. Somehow, it was not as much fun for the Republicans once he made that statement. Parade chants continued, such as "Ma, ma, where's my Pa? Gone to the White House, ha, ha, ha," but this proved not to be crippling. On both sides, these exchanges probably did not move that many voters. Again, people in those days tended to be born into one party or the other and were loyal to their heritage.

There were also two minor parties, the Greenback Party and the Prohibition Party. Neither was very strong, but both were anti-Blaine and anti-Republican. Moreover, according to expert estimates, the votes they received in New York tended to detract more from Blaine than from Cleveland. Nevertheless, the election looked very close. Both sides were worried, which was a good sign. Still, Blaine suffered one final blow barely a week before the election. On 29 October 1884, a large number of Protestant clergymen held a rally for Blaine at a New York hotel. Several of them made short addresses, one of whom was a Presbyterian minister named Samuel Burchard. Burchard's remarks were pretty commonplace, and there was a lot of buzzing. Blaine was tired and did not pay much attention. A reporter, however, picked out a key sentence from Burchard's comments that said, "We are Republicans and don't propose to leave our party and identify ourselves with the party whose antecedents have been rum, Romanism, and rebellion." This statement hurt Blaine because in New York City the Irish vote was very large and New York's political organizers and ward bosses were strongly Irish, most belonging to Tammany. For a Republican, however, Blaine had been unusually successful in getting Irish support. Irish in New York tended to vote Democratic. Hence, Burchard's reference to rum and Romanism was too much.

The Democrats immediately printed thousands of flyers and delivered them to the Catholic churches on the following Sunday, where they were handed out to the congregations. It is difficult to say what the specific effect was, but it was bound to cost some votes at a time when there were no votes to spare. In the end, the election turned on New York State, and Grover Cleveland won by 1,149 votes out of over a million cast. A shift in New York State of 600 votes would have elected Blaine. When elections are that close, any arbitrarily selected factor—such as Conkling, the mugwumps, or Burchard's gaff—might be said to be the determining one. Any one of those factors could have lost Blaine 600 votes. In the end, Blaine failed to win the election because he was unlucky. Had he been lucky, he would have won. That election ended Blaine's presidential aspirations.

Some critics have seen Blaine's career as one long quest for the presidency, which is not true. He had real interest in party management. Gilded Age historian H. Wayne Morgan calls him a superb party manager. The shaping and direction of the party were dearer to him than any other single thing. He had a deep interest in foreign policy, and in my opinion, he was a bold innovator and precursor. Blaine's significance in foreign policy, however, is disputed by many of my colleagues.

James Blaine is remembered largely for the horse race stories. His charm, magnetism, and charisma, which were so legendary, died with him. Not much is heard about James Blaine the man. Instead, people are more familiar with the two-dimensional cardboard cutouts of Gilded Age politicians like Blaine, who are dismissed as fat men with mustaches and nothing particular to say, a very wrong view. James Blaine was unique in his day, and he is well worth rediscovering in ours.

QUESTION: What is the cause for our rediscovery of Blaine 100 years later?

MR. HEALY: One reason is renewed interest in the Gilded Age, perhaps because of a parallel between our politics now and politics then. As in the Gilded Age, there is much uncertainty today about what direction the government is headed. It looks messy. Historians have recently taken figures from the Gilded Age more seriously, and once taken seriously, Blaine becomes a major figure. People like myself who are interested in diplomacy and foreign relations look at and constantly return to Blaine because however one evaluates him, he is one of the big nexuses of dispute. What one thinks of Blaine is somewhat of a touchstone for what one thinks about other aspects of international policy in the Gilded Age. There has been a great deal of interest in Blaine, much of it negative. Some good scholars do not like him, scholars such as Robert Beisner, Justus Doenecke, and to some extent, David Pletcher, for whose opinion I have an enormous regard. In the other camp, there are those like me, who stress his creative side.

A good case for and against Blaine can be made both ways. In the end Blaine continues to receive attention because he is important.

QUESTION: What was Blaine's activity in the Civil War?

MR. HEALY: Blaine was only 31 when the Civil War began, but he already had a wife and children, and clearly he did not think it was best to go. On the whole, this decision was not much of a handicap. The feeling at the time was that a married man in his 30s with children was not really required to go. He vigorously cultivated the Grand Army of the Republic (GAR) and Unionist sentiment. Ironically, he was a Lincoln Republican and very moderate about reconstruction in the actual Reconstruction period until it was ending. As a more ambitious figure, he "waved the bloody shirt" and exploited lingering wartime passions to appeal to Union veterans.

QUESTION: Did Blaine's political ambitions affect the conduct of his foreign policy while he was secretary of state? Presumably, he would have liked to earn some major diplomatic achievements to put on his record. For example, did Blaine's ambitions have any bearing on U.S. Latin American policy that you mentioned or on his inclination or disinclination to take risks in events such as the War of the Pacific?

MR. HEALY: Blaine was inherently a risk-taker. He was bold and willing to take a gamble on occasion. Obviously, some relationship existed between his political position and his attempts at foreign policy, particularly in the Garfield administration. When the Garfield administration came into office, Roscoe Conkling, who was feeling endangered in New York, demanded total control of New York patronage. Garfield wanted to keep the peace and give him enough to keep him happy, but he did not want to turn over everything; moreover, with Blaine being an enemy and in the administration, the situation soon led to all-out war between the Garfield administration and Conkling, who was ultimately driven out of the Senate with his career broken. As a result, many Republicans became angry at Blaine at the same time that the Democrats were furiously anti-Blaine, and everything that Blaine did came under a storm of abuse and criticism.

There are some criticisms that are legitimate. His attempt to intervene in the War of the Pacific was ineptly done and produced a fiasco, which was itself grounds for considerable criticism. Instead of attacking him on those grounds, however, his enemies accused him of trying to profiteer through his association with a bond scheme to take over the Peruvian treasury and pay an indemnity to Chile instead of giving territory. Blaine had been interested in the scheme because he was trying to prevent territorial transfer, but he was not personally mixed up in any of it. Time after time, Blaine would be accused of wrongdoing even when his actions were not connected to any kind of economic benefit to himself. The criticism and accusations consequently made it harder to gain support in Congress, though Blaine could be very successful with Republicans in Congress. The picture just became more complicated. Blaine was always fighting his domestic battles at the same time that he was trying to carry out foreign policy.

QUESTION: What about the speakership as a route to the presidency?

MR. HEALY: The speakership certainly can give a person prominence. On the whole, it has not been one of the main routes to the White House or to the nomination, but neither is it a hindrance.

QUESTION: Do you agree that the best road to the White House historically has been the vice presidency?

MR. HEALY: Definitely. About a quarter of all vice presidents have become presidents. That statistic indicates that any vice president will have about one chance in four of becoming president. It does not necessarily happen that way, but the percentages are good.

QUESTION: What is the reason for the amazingly strong factional loyalty that allowed someone like Blaine to pick his man and have the entire organization accept that candidacy? Was it simple patronage?

MR. HEALY: Blaine is rather special in this aspect. Not many people could manage that feat. Everyone who talks or writes about Blaine as a contemporary stresses his incredible magnetism and charm. On the other hand, there must have been another side to him because so many people hated him. Like Franklin Roosevelt, one hears about how he could charm everyone, but at the same time many people remained uncharmed. Blaine followers were personally loyal to Blaine in large numbers. Also, Blaine did control a large block of Republicans, which is one of the things that made him such a power for so long. He could deliver in a way that is hard to parallel. He did not have all of the good quotes and clever remarks, but by common testimony he had great presence and amiability. He knew how to put people at ease. He had a fantastic memory for faces and people, as well as for all kinds of political data. As usual, this talent was matched by lack of memory in other areas. All kinds of stories circulated about how absentminded he was. For example, he supposedly fired the gardener and then asked on the next day why the work was not done. He would mislay his checks and become angry at the bank for not having them. His personal impact was enormous, but these kinds of stories are hard to come by except by testimony.

As far as his eloquence, he gave Garfield's eulogy in Congress, and the last paragraph of that eulogy is very beautiful.

QUESTION: Would you elaborate on a few particular charges of corruption that may have been true? If true, were they significant?

MR. HEALY: The longest running and most weighted scandal was the one concerning the Mulligan letters, but there was never proof of anything illegal. Some of Blaine's defenders have made exactly this point. For example, Norman Tutorow wrote a book about Blaine and the presidency in which he asks how some historians are allowed to make such claims when there is never any proof of illegality. I personally am convinced that Blaine had his shady side and that he benefited financially from doing favors for corporations and rich men by conscious agreement.

What I am saying may sound like whitewash. Some of the things Blaine did were ethically bad. It just does not seem right to single Blaine out when others did the same things. For example, no one worries about Daniel Webster taking retainers every year from the Maine interests, but Blaine gets repeatedly criticized for doing the same thing.

In the end, without hard proof it is hard to know what to say. With all that smoke, there is likely to have been fire. We do know that he was doing favors for corporations in exchange for certain rewards. His own correspondence tells us this fact, and there is some rather compromising stuff. He writes one large operator that he is ready to be of use and that he knows the man will appreciate it. What exactly he did that was useful or what he received for his service I do not know, however.

NARRATOR: Your presentation has been penetrating and incisive, and we thank you, Professor Healy, for sharing your substantial knowledge.

II

THE PASSING OF THE MODERN PRESIDENCY: STATESMEN WHO FELL SHORT

CHAPTER THREE

Robert Taft*

WILLIAM WEMPLE AND KENNETH W. THOMPSON

NARRATOR: William Wemple graduated from Harvard College in 1934 and Columbia University Law School in 1937. He became a partner of Dewey, Ballantine, Bushby, Palmer, and Wood in 1952 and is now a retired partner. He is a Fellow of the American Bar Foundation; a member of the American Bar Association's banking and business law section; a member of the American Law Institute; and a past chairman of the banking, corporation, and business law section of the New York State Bar Association. Mr. Wemple is a longtime friend and supporter of the Miller Center. Kenneth Thompson is director of the Miller Center.

MR. WEMPLE: My last presentation at the Miller Center was about the meteoric political career of Wendell Willkie. He was the Republican Party's nominee for president in 1940. He was also a former Democrat, a staunch admirer of Newton D. Baker, with an almost religious faith in the League of Nations.

Senator Robert Taft of Ohio was a totally different political figure. Taft tried four times to get the Republican Party's

---

Presented in a Forum at the Miller Center of Public Affairs on 19 April 1995.

nomination for president but never quite succeeded. He was a son of William Howard Taft, who was president from 1908 to 1912.

In the disorderly party politics of this country, Robert Taft managed to keep a strong grip on the loyalty of Republican Party voters in Ohio throughout his entire career. He grew up and lived in a suburb of Cincinnati and practiced law in the Cincinnati firm of Taft, Stettinius and Hollister. He soon went into politics, like practically everyone else in Ohio. In referring to rough-and-tumble party politics, I think particularly of what an English visitor to Cincinnati, then a frontier town, said about Americans in the 1830s. She cautioned her countrymen against disturbing their established habits and solid principles by introducing the jarring tumult and universal degradation that result from placing all of the power of the state in the hands of the populace. That visitor was Frances Trollope, who wrote this assessment of American politics in her book, *Domestic Manners of the Americans.*

Robert Taft was no ordinary politician. He not only did his homework, but with almost no exceptions, he spoke his mind regardless of political consequences. His loyal Republican voters obviously valued that quality, probably above all others. The Great Depression not only failed to change that; it even emphasized it.

Taft's biographer noted that characteristic and paid it tribute, but he could not refrain from comments that have a populist flavor. He noted, for example, Taft's hard-headed urging of a shortened foreclosure delay before the state could sell property for nonpayment of taxes. This characteristic showed Taft's least attractive quality: budget consciousness to the point of being callous to the human dimensions of the economic crisis.

That, however, was the nature of the man. He served in the U.S. Senate from his first election in 1938 until his death in 1953. His reelection in 1950 was by a landslide vote against the Democratic candidate, Joseph Ferguson, who had made the fatal mistake of debating the issues with Taft.

It is understandable that Taft probably could never have unseated Franklin Roosevelt in the days of the New Deal and then World War II. It is less clear, however, why he never succeeded in even getting the Republican nomination. The most likely explanation is that the most influential Republican Party leaders did not think he could win. They may have been right. Taft refused to alter any of his most important beliefs and to refrain from speaking his mind about them. Knowing that it might cost him votes made no difference to him. Taft also had an aversion to the usual varieties of politicking, such as attending large gatherings, shaking hands, and engaging in small talk.

Although Taft found the causes of the Great Depression baffling, his biographer was unable to resist interpreting Taft's confusion socialistically. He argued that Taft's analysis of the causes was one-sided and ignored such factors as gross inequities in personal income. Taft *was* scathingly critical of Franklin Roosevelt's New Deal, but selectively. Although he considered Roosevelt a devious and demagogic showman, he accepted the necessity of relief and public works, the minimum wage law, child-labor laws, federal unemployment insurance, and old-age pensions. His most critical invective was directed at New Deal deficit spending and the concentration of ever-increasing governing power in the executive branch and its growing bureaucracy. He found the National Recovery Administration (NRA) and the Agricultural Adjustment Administration (AAA) especially obnoxious because they tried to regulate prices.

In 1938 Taft won election to the U.S. Senate. In this endeavor he was greatly helped by persuading the Democratic candidate, Robert Bulkley of Cleveland to debate the issues with him. Within a year of his entry into office, Taft plunged right into the Senate's business. He denounced the New Deal spending and deficit financing. When Roosevelt mockingly challenged him to show how the budget could be balanced, he stepped up to the task, declaring that the $9 billion budget could be cut by $7 billion by eliminating waste, abolishing conflicting agencies, and slashing funds for relief and for farmers. Most of all, Taft argued that the government could reduce spending simply by *wanting* to reduce spending. If higher taxes were needed, so be it. His criticism of farm subsidies was indicative of his general approach to politics: (1) do the homework, (2) decide what needs to be done, then (3) move full steam ahead and damn the torpedoing of some votes.

In May 1940 Taft made the first of several radio addresses in which he urged the United States to stay out of the European war and stated that New Deal spending should be stopped or drastically slowed, that national defense should be our first priority, and that Congress should form a joint committee to oversee a plan providing for adequate defense. He said that our joining in the war would be more likely to destroy democracy in the United States than to destroy German dictatorship.

Taft's biographer emphasized the damage these speeches did to Taft's campaign for the nomination. Taft was aware of this, however, and made them anyway. He strongly believed that the United States should stay out of the war and that the Roosevelt administration was campaigning to get us in, which was undoubtedly true. Taft's speeches may have been a crucial factor in keeping us out of the war so long. He agreed with aiding the Allies, but only to the extent of repealing the Neutrality Act so that the British could use their ample resources to buy munitions on a cash-and-carry basis, the same as any belligerent.

Taft was a rare breed of U.S. politicians—immune to the emotions and rhetoric of war and to the predominant wish to give all possible aid to the Allies even at the risk of war.

In 1936 Taft had been Ohio's favorite-son candidate in the primary for the Republican nomination for president. At the convention, however, Alfred Landon had a lead from the start, prompting Taft to withdraw his bid and second him. Taft's misfortunes in seeking the Republican nomination continued in 1940, when the convention nominated Wendell Willkie. In 1944, Taft won reelection to the Senate in a tight race. His presidential aspirations were once again dashed in that year, though, as Dewey garnered a sizeable advantage in the national convention. Once again, as in 1940, the eastern internationalist wing of the Republican Party won out over the more conservative Midwestern wing.

Taft had begun to find Dewey arrogant. He also did not trust the Easterners, whom he considered too internationalist. He ridiculed the world federalists as impractical or worse and denounced calls for a world military alliance. He endorsed the U.N. Charter as at least better than a military alliance or an international state.

The year 1948 probably should have been Taft's year to be nominated by the Republicans, but Dewey's well-organized forces again captured the nomination in the convention. Taft's last try was 1952. The Eastern internationalists of the party, however, had found their ideal candidate in the war hero, General Dwight D. Eisenhower. Taft again came close but failed to win the nomination.

This time the party did nominate a winner. Ike was enormously popular, winning the election in a landslide. The country also voted in Republican majorities in both the House and the Senate, making Taft the Senate majority leader. In the Franklin Roosevelt years, of course, it is unlikely that any Republican nominee could have won the election. After FDR's death, Truman managed a remarkable upset victory over Dewey in 1948. That year, or possibly 1952, might well have been the one time that Taft could have been elected had he been nominated.

The midterm elections of 1994 have certainly confirmed that strong support for much of Taft's political philosophy exists today, more so than at any time in Taft's political career. Taft was never an enthusiastic enough interventionist to satisfy the eastern internationalists of that time, though he did finally support NATO. He never did like stationing troops abroad, however. In that respect and others, Taft would have had much company today that he did not have in his own time.

A Footnote on Robert A. Taft

Kenneth W. Thompson

From his early years, Bob Taft was known for his reticence and reserve. Even a girlfriend chided him, calling him a "human safety valve of enthusiasm." It cannot have been easy growing up in the White House, but one friend observed that it merely left him as reserved as before. The headings in an excellent biography by James T. Patterson that describes his youth are: "A Striving Boy," "The Struggle for Self-Control," "Avoiding the Limelight," "days of Drift and Deference," and "Finding Himself." He grew up and lived in the shadow of his father—President William Howard Taft— and his grandfather Alphonso, who was secretary of war and attorney general in the Grant administration. For the grandfather, the requirements for the young were unambiguous: The model young man was a character of sobriety, industry, and integrity without blemish who should never cease to put his best effort forward. Alphonso was stern, upright, and forever industrious. By contrast, William Taft had some qualities in common with his father but none of his austerity. There was a twinkle in his eye and an infectious laugh. For Robert, however, his father's attitude was one of cool observation. The President made clear that he did not believe in coddling and that mediocrity would never do. His letters to Robert were full of admonitions, and the son dutifully responded. He was first in his class academically at Taft, Yale, and Harvard Law School but not in sociability. He minimized his success, saying that all that was needed to achieve such a record was the ability to memorize and learn by rote. At the time, these abilities were his greatest strength. His father was commissioner in the Philippines. The faculty toured Europe. From these experiences, young Bob resolved to save Asia from communism, but no particular part of Europe. This attitude was reflected later in his isolationist view of Europe. He was opposed to intervening to turn back Hitler in the

1930s and 1940s and was an opponent of NATO after World War II.

His biographer admits that these simple clues from childhood of what the man was to become may not add up, but the fact is he reveled in solitary pursuits. He volunteered for military service in World War I but was rejected not once but several times. He was troubled by not serving because as he said, he would always have to explain. Some would look down on him for failing to do his duty. He did not appeal his rejections for military service, however, but at the invitation of Herbert Hoover joined the Ford administration in Washington and later the American Relief Administration in Paris. He was close enough to events in Versailles and Paris to be critical of the quest for a peace treaty. Like Hoover, Taft reacted against what he described as the diplomatic intrigue of Clemenceau and Lloyd George. He supported his father's belief in a League of Nations but insisted that it must be confined to two functions: the prevention of war and the legal definition of what constitutes an aggressive war. He eventually accepted Henry Cabot Lodge's reservations to the Covenant in the Senate. For him, peace was possible not through settling disputes by force or accommodation, but by judicial tribunals.

The next stage in his career came when he returned to Cincinnati. For no clearly defined reason, he decided to run for the state assembly. He led nine candidates on the Republican slate from Hamilton county and soon made his influence felt in Columbus. Once again, observers noted his pattern of making his way alone. He shunned intimacy with strangers and reacted negatively to their comments connecting him with his father. His wife remained in Cincinnati and from Monday through Thursday he ate alone in the hotel in Columbus. He generally voted for the program of the Republican governor, but he also tended to vote on the issues as he saw them. He introduced a bill to elect judges on a nonpartisan basis. He joined a bipartisan majority in support of a minimum wage bill for women, but it was killed in the Senate. He favored bills for an increase of mothers' pensions and a measure to grant workmen's compensation. He favored a constitutional amendment against the use of child labor. His greatest accomplishment was in facing up to the state's and cities' financial problem through a carefully constructed series of tax increases. Consistent with his past and despite his electoral victories, he developed no close personal relations with anyone in three terms in the state legislature. Because of his competence as a majority leader, however, he was elected Speaker.

In his quest for the presidency, Taft ran as Ohio's favorite son in the May 1936 presidential primary. When it was clear that Governor Alfred M. Landon of Kansas would win on the first ballot, the Ohio delegation was eager to leave Taft and throw their ballot to Landon. Thus, Taft withdrew his name and seconded Landon's nomination. The campaign was heated at times, and Taft contributed, saying that "if Roosevelt [Franklin Delano] was not a Communist today, he was bound to become one." Taft admitted to a friend that he had just been making reactionary speeches. He held then and throughout his career to a literal interpretation of the law and the Constitution, which was one pillar of his thinking. The second pillar was his opposition to the enhancement of executive power over that of the Congress and the courts. He anticipated victory for Landon and predicted that he would carry Cincinnati by 5,000 votes. Instead, Roosevelt carried it by 44,000, as well as most of the nine county officers and two out of three of Hamilton's county's state senate officers. The country had witnessed a political revolution. Roosevelt had attracted millions of underprivileged voters. America had changed, but Bob Taft had not.

Taft's next run for the office came in 1940. Safe in his Senate seat until 1944, it is a fair question to ask, why would he try again so soon after 1936? His answer might have been that he had a famous name. He had been raised to excel. Could history not repeat itself and a Taft succeed a Roosevelt? His first task was to secure Ohio, and he managed to negotiate with Governor John Bricker, who agreed not to run until 1944, an arrangement neither side ever confirmed. Perhaps it occurred, because a Gallup poll showed the senator with a 62 to 38 advantage over the governor. By February and before the first primary (he avoided primaries whenever he could), Taft had visited 28 states and made 40 major speeches. He stressed the healing of minor divisions within Ohio, as when opposition arose to the selection of Congressman Clarence Brown as delegate-at-large or when feuding broke out with

Congressman George Bender of Cleveland. He also sought to enlist various groups in his cause, as when he declared: "We ought to get Joe Louis on our side." He gained a measure of support from the media. In January, *Time* placed him on its cover. Walter Lippmann wrote of Taft's saving grace of intellectual humility. Yet Taft suffered from an image problem. He was impressive in small groups, but his speeches failed to strike a spark. He spoke as if he were submitting a brief in a probate case. His handlers tried to humanize him. He resented his coverage by the mass media; the negative image went from bad to worse. Surprisingly, it did not affect substantially his standing in the polls. His other problem was foreign policy. He tried to minimize its importance, but Hitler made that effort impossible. Whenever possible, he changed the subject to the New Deal. Its totalitarian ideas, he said, were the threat, not the Nazis. At first he was against any form of involvement in Europe. He modified his view by saying that the United States would fight if Hitler sought to gain a foothold in the Western Hemisphere. Beyond that acquiescence, Taft would not go all of the time, protesting that he was not an isolationist. His main weaknesses in 1940 were his image, despite warnings from Republicans such as Landon, and his foreign policy.

Taft lost on the sixth ballot at the Republican Convention. According to the polls before the convention, Republican voters gave Thomas Dewey more than 50 percent of the vote, with Taft and Vandenberg trailing. By late April, Willkie's name appeared for the first time, and by late May he had passed Taft. By convention time, Willkie had replaced Dewey in the lead. The public and the media had grown uneasy about Taft, and Lippmann compared him with Neville Chamberlain, predicting a national disaster if he were elected. Once the convention began, 5,000 Willkie supporters also filled the galleries and began the chant, "We want Willkie." Dewey was in the lead on the first and second ballots, while Taft returned a narrow lead for second. On the fourth ballot, Willkie took the lead, and Taft moved ahead of Dewey by four votes. On the fifth ballot, Dewey's support collapsed, and Willkie remained in the lead, with 429 votes to Taft's 377. On the sixth ballot, the Michigan delegates were polled and gave Willkie 35 votes and Taft only two. Other states followed, including Virginia, which gave Willkie 16 votes for 502. Taft told himself after the struggle "never again" and kept that promise until 1948. Looking back, there were "might have beens" in the Taft entourage. If the convention had been told in April instead of on 24 June, the result might have been different. If he had taken a more moderate stand on the war in Europe, if Hoover had released his delegates, or if Taft had not been overwhelmed in New England, New Jersey, Delaware and Maryland, where Willkie's margin was 194 to 23, he might have had a chance. His advantage of 103 to 58 in the South and 114 to 53 in the Midwest. He lost because of a lusterless image and the feeling among voters around the country that he could not defeat FDR. All of these factors having been acknowledged, he came amazingly close, closer than in any other campaign.

In 1948, the race was between Taft and Dewey. The media presented a more evenhanded picture of Taft than in earlier elections. His speeches revealed a more personal touch, although even the more favorable columnists continued to describe him as shy and deferential. Taft enlisted the help of the public relations profession, but none of there efforts had had much effect in past because their attempts to portray him as a moderate clashed with the style of his Ohio team of campaigners, especially the campaign chairman, Charles Brown. Brown spurned the envoys of Governor Stassen, who talked of a coalition against Dewey and refused to allow Brown, Taft, or other moderates to have any part in the campaign. Stassen had won primaries in Nebraska and Wisconsin and had challenged Taft for 23 of Ohio's 53 conservative seats. Taft returned from Washington, and from 17 April to 4 May he campaigned almost desperately to reverse inroads on the vote that Stassen appeared to be making. He managed to hold Stassen to victories for only nine of the delegates, but James Reston wrote that one more victory of this kind would be the undoing of both candidates.

The 1948 Republican convention was held in Philadelphia. From the first maneuvers, the greater skill of Dewey's professional campaign manager, Herbert Brownell, was evident. Despite an alliance with Stassen, Taft lost a challenge to the composition of the Georgia delegation and failed to gain any ground on Dewey in other strategic maneuvers. In the balloting, Dewey on the first ballot had 434 votes to Taft's 224 with 548 required for a majority. On the second ballot, Dewey increased to 515 and Taft to 274. Before the third ballot and following a recess, Governor Bricker read a statement from Taft acknowledging defeat. The convention went on to choose Earl Warren of California as his running mate. Some explained the results by saying that Taft in contrast with Dewey had been unwilling to make promises to attract support as Brownell had allegedly done with Martin of Pennsylvania, Kean of Missouri, and Halleck, all well-known right-wingers. Those with whom Taft might have bargained, however, including Warren, Stassen, and Vandenberg found Taft's foreign policy views unacceptable and questioned his ability to win. Taft remained a largely regional candidate with strength mainly in the Midwest, the South, and Texas. Although he complained privately about the New Deal press and critical defections, he recognized that many believed he was unelectable.

His last, some said his best, chance came in 1952. He had been reelected to the Senate. His wife's depression prompted the decision to handle most of his correspondence and dictation from home. He kept up his criticism of foreign policy but was less uncompromising on domestic policy. He joined with Hubert Humphrey invalidating 3,000 or more elections under the Taft-Hartley Act, which had been invalidated because it had not been preceded by the signing of anti-Communist affidavits. He made concessions to farm interests, began to edge away from Senator Joseph McCarthy, and in other ways protected himself against charges of being a reactionary. It was agreed by most commentators that the 1952 campaign was the least organized of Taft's four attempts.

He recruited professional politicians, such as Congressman Carroll Reece of Tennessee; John D. M. Hamilton, a former GOP national chairman; and Thomas E. Coleman, who was Mr. Republican of Wisconsin. While valuable additions, these advisers did not broaden the spectrum of politics in Taft's team. Instead, because they were all on the right, they weakened Taft's own political instinct to expand his political base, which had always been a problem. For example, a Gallup poll in August 1951 found that five out of six Republicans had positive views of him, but more than half of independent voters were negative. Only 20 percent thought he would make a good president, while 27 percent said he would not. Once again, Taft's strength was with party regulars and Republican senators while Eisenhower was strong with party rank and file, Independents, and Democrats. Taft understood this whether he acknowledged it or not.

The struggle for the nomination went through various stages. At first Taft disparaged Eisenhower's qualifications, but at a later stage he pointed to the similarity of their views even in foreign policy. After the first part of 1952, he set out on a furious campaign schedule. Someone calculated that he had made 550 speeches, traveled 50,000 miles, and was seen by two million people. The start of the primary season was not auspicious for Taft. In New Hampshire, Eisenhower received more votes than the other three candidates combined, including Taft. The general also took Texas, Minnesota, and New Jersey. Taft came back in Wisconsin, Nebraska, and Illinois, while Eisenhower won Massachusetts. Taft rallied to gain Ohio and won in state conventions in West Virginia, North Dakota, and Wyoming. Eisenhower came back in Oregon, Rhode Island, and Vermont. Taft's strategy was one of continual adjustments and readjustment to the changing realities of the campaign. For example, he tried to strengthen his position for the Wisconsin primary by seeking the endorsement of Senator Joseph McCarthy. The endorsement, however, was never forthcoming. He immersed himself the foreign policy literature, partly because criticism had mounted not only concerning his policy views, but even his integrity. As he approached the convention, he had 462 committed delegates and Eisenhower had 389. To gain the nomination, he needed 604 delegates.

Two events in effect determined the election. The first was the struggle over the delegates in Texas. The second was the debate on the recognition of the delegates in the convention itself. On the first, history repeated itself much as the Republican convention credentials committee in 1912 had settled an earlier controversy by seating party regulars favorable to William Howard Taft. Theodore Roosevelt attacked the action as a "steamroller" and walked out of the convention. He created the Progressive Party and in splitting the Republican vote contributed to the election of Woodrow Wilson. History repeated itself in 1952, and a bitter debate ensued between the supporters of Taft and Eisenhower. Four thousand met in Mineral Wells outside of Fort Worth. The regulars announced that the vote was 762 to 222 for Taft, with between 30 and 34 of 38 convention delegates for Taft. The Eisenhower forces walked out.

Thereafter, a parliamentary ruling decided the nomination in Chicago. In the maneuvering, Brownell and the Eisenhower team overwhelmed Clarence Brown and the Republicans. An early test vote revealed the numerical superiority of Ike over Taft. The Taft forces had hoped to gain momentum, but the test vote showed Ike's greater strength.

One other deciding factor goes back to a personal observation. I stood on Michigan Avenue and watched the two candidate arrive. Taft stood in the back of his limousine but barely moved his arms, which he held aloft locked in a frozen posture. Ike's demeanor was buoyant, vital, and personal as he drove past the crowd. Even in the state that had voted for Taft—Illinois—Ike was clearly the crowd favorite.

Earlier I had testified on foreign policy before the Republican platform committee. One impression lingered as I left the hearing room. The dominant personalities on the committee—senators Nixon, Ives, and others—were clearly Eisenhower men. That night John Foster Dulles flew in with a draft of the foreign policy statement. Clearly, Ike had the stronger voice in the participants in that committee. Eisenhower had overcome Taft. Cries of "stealing the vote" subsided. Not long thereafter, following a historic meeting on Morningside Heights of the two statesmen and their cooperation in the early months of the Eisenhower administration, Bob Taft passed away never having reached his ultimate goal.

CHAPTER FOUR

Senator Mike Mansfield*

GREGORY A. OLSON

NARRATOR: Gregory Olson, who is assistant professor in the field of communication studies at Marquette University, has a position in the Department of Communication at the University of Wisconsin, Oshkosh. He has also taught at Eastern Montana College, the University of Wisconsin at River Falls, Regis College in Denver, and the University of Minnesota, where he received his doctorate in speech communication in 1988. His dissertation was titled, "Mike Mansfield's Ethos in the Evolution of U.S. Policy in Indochina." He earned his master's degree in communication at the University of Wisconsin at Superior in 1972 and his bachelor's degree in education, majoring in history, at the University of Wisconsin at Oshkosh in 1969.

Mr. Olson is the author of *Mansfield and Vietnam: A Study in Rhetorical Adaptation* (1995). He has also published a chapter in a recent book about President Eisenhower entitled "Eisenhower and the Indochina Problem." For this and other research, he has received grants and awards for research in the archives of former presidents Lyndon Johnson, Richard Nixon, Gerald Ford, and Dwight Eisenhower, as well as former Senator Mike Mansfield. He

---

Presented in a Forum at the Miller Center of Public Affairs on 30 May 1996.

has presented research papers at national conferences and is currently conducting research on four different papers on Mike Mansfield to be presented at professional meetings. In addition, Mr. Olson has served as a commentator for the media throughout Wisconsin on the subject of presidential debates, the Vietnam War, and Senator Mansfield. He is a member of several professional organizations in his field.

Mike Mansfield was clearly regarded by senior senators as a "member of the club," but he was also an independent leader who was widely respected. Today Mr. Olson will discuss Senator Mansfield's career, particularly the question of what kept him from being seriously considered as a presidential candidate.

MR. OLSON: Mansfield was probably more popular with Republicans in the Senate than he was with Democrats, and it certainly made him a unique kind of majority leader. Many scholars writing about the Senate agree that after Lyndon Johnson left the Senate to become vice president in 1961, his domineering leadership style simply would not work anymore. Indeed, Mansfield was a radical departure from the Johnson model. Former Senator William Proxmire (D-Wisconsin) once wrote, "Mansfield transformed the Senate from a wimpish body of 'yes' men under Johnson to an effective Parliamentary democracy."* I recently finished an oral history project on Mansfield which suggested that he may have had more ambition than is commonly thought and perhaps even private thoughts of the presidency. One cannot find that information in most of the public record. Most people who are writing about Mansfield are amazed that this high-ranking senator did not seem

---

*All cites are taken from the following three sources: Olson, Gregory A., "Mike Mansfield's Ethos in the Evolution of United States Policy in Indochina" (Ph.D. dissertation, University of Minnesota, 1988); Olson, Gregory A. *Mansfield and Vietnam: A Study in Rhetorical Adaptation* (East Lansing: Michigan State University Press); and Valeo, Francis R., Oral History Interviews with Donald A. Ritchie, Senate Historical Office, Washington, D.C., 1985–86.

to have much of an ego nor any ambition beyond being a senator from Montana. It takes quite a bit of ambition to get even that far.

Edmund Muskie once said that "people don't remember great Majority Leaders over the long haul." Michael J. Mansfield—who served in the position from 1961 to 1976, longer than any leader in history—appears to prove Muskie's contention. Robert Peabody speculated that little has been written about Mansfield because of his "laconic, low-keyed style of operation" and because he "never sought higher office." The only book that has been published about Mansfield is mine. Peabody's assertion is borne out when comparing Johnson to Mansfield. LBJ was hardly "laconic" or "low-keyed" in style, and he eagerly sought higher office. If Peabody was correct, Mansfield's style and lack of ambition for the White House may help to explain why those who write on the position of majority leader always analyze Johnson but Mansfield is often ignored. Scholars tend to skip Mansfield and go on to Robert Byrd, and sometimes they even miss Byrd.

Mansfield probably never considered a run for the presidency. He often said, "The Senate was the achievement of my highest ambition." His career supports that claim. Those seeking the presidency often consider the vice presidency as part of that larger quest, and Nixon, Kennedy, Johnson, Humphrey, Muskie, Ford, Mondale, Dole, and Bush are all contemporary examples. On three separate occasions Mansfield was considered for the vice-presidential nomination. What may be unique about Mansfield is that he expressed no interest in that position and turned down those offers. In fact, he did not even want to become Senate whip in 1956. He told LBJ that he would much rather concentrate on his foreign relations committee assignment; his interest in the Far East was a major focus throughout his career. Southerners did not want Humphrey to be whip during the civil rights battles, and they found Mansfield more acceptable because as a Westerner he opposed cloture and was generally well liked. Mansfield thus became whip. This position eventually led him to become the Senate majority leader, which he also seemed to resist.

His first chance at a vice-presidential nomination was not much of a chance. I have found only two sources that indicate that in 1956 he was mentioned as a possible "Catholic" running mate for

Adlai Stevenson. The nomination eventually went to Estes Kefauver. Mansfield supported Kennedy in that contest at the Democratic convention. Shortly afterward, Johnson wrote the following in a letter to Mansfield:

> In thinking back over the Convention, one of the things that stands out and pleases me very, very much is my personal knowledge that there are men like Mike Mansfield who infinitely prefer to be a good Senator instead of Vice-President. You know I happened to feel exactly that way about being Senate Majority Leader.

Johnson, who changed his mind when Kennedy extended the vice-presidential offer to him in 1960, expected Mansfield to do the same thing. In 1964 Johnson began to play the game of suggesting other potential vice-presidential candidates, even though Humphrey was considered to be the front-runner. Robert Kennedy was mentioned, as was Sargent Shriver, Robert McNamara, other Cabinet members, Robert Wagner (then mayor of New York), Adlai Stevenson, and senators Eugene McCarthy, Thomas Dodd, Edmund Muskie, and Mansfield. Humphrey and possibly McCarthy as a long shot were probably the most serious candidates. In July 1964, *Time* magazine listed several reasons why Mansfield might have been appealing as a vice-presidential candidate. I am not sure he would have been a good presidential candidate because he lacked charisma. Johnson may not have been charismatic either, but when a vice president inherits the presidency as he did, it makes a future presidential candidacy easier.

While many people felt that Johnson was playing games with his choice of vice president, Rowland Evans and Robert Novak think that he was serious about Mansfield. They speculate that Johnson might have wanted to replace Mansfield as majority leader with Hubert Humphrey, who was more aggressive and skillful in Johnson's mind. Interestingly, John Kennedy had said to his aide, Kenneth O'Donnell, in 1960 that one of the reasons he wanted Johnson as his vice president was to get Mansfield as his majority leader instead of Johnson. William White, who often "sailed a kite" for Johnson, is the person who came up with the trial balloon rumor right before the 1964 convention. Johnson said to O'Donnell:

> I've decided on Mike Mansfield. . . . Kenny, you can't be against Mansfield, . . . you nor any of the Kennedy people. He's one of you. You admire him and respect him. If you're thinking of Bobby running in 1972, he's no problem. He'll be too old to run then.

When O'Donnell suggested that Mansfield would not accept the nomination, Johnson said:

> That's what they said about old Lyndon Johnson in 1960. But when they lead you up on that mountain, and show you those green fields down below and that beautiful White House standing there—you know what you do? You take it. They all take it.

A number of years later, O'Donnell had an opportunity to ask Mansfield about it, and Mansfield replied:

> I, too, saw White's column, and like everybody else in Washington I knew what it meant. I waited a while, and then I decided to beat Lyndon to the punch. I went to the White House and said to him, "Mr. President, I saw Mr. White's article about me in the newspaper, and I want you to know that under no circumstances will I ever accept the nomination as Vice-President." That ended that.

This story is the generally accepted version of the events.

In his autobiography, Humphrey shed more light on the trial balloon idea. I asked Johnson's adviser, George Reedy, who is a colleague of mine at Marquette, whether Humphrey had in fact already been decided on by that time. Reedy replied that he thought so, but Johnson liked to play games. He added that polls showed that the vice-presidential selection would have made little difference, so Johnson was free to choose whomever he wanted. Jack Valenti agreed with that assessment in an oral history he did. Senator Frank Lausche (D-Ohio) wrote a nice letter to Mansfield indicating that some people wished that he would consider the vice-presidential nomination.

While Johnson may never have intended to formally invite Mansfield onto the 1964 ticket, George McGovern did intend to do so. In December 1971, McGovern wrote a letter urging Mansfield not to endorse anyone because McGovern believed that he was in good shape to win the nomination. This conviction proved to be true. Mansfield would never have endorsed anyone anyway. He would not even endorse people to be his whip, and he ended up with whips who were philosophically different from him. He would not endorse Edward Kennedy over Byrd, and he would not endorse John Pastore (D-Rhode Island) over Russell Long (D-Louisiana) earlier, which is one thing about his leadership style that political scientists often criticize. He said that he tried to make the Senate a place where each senator was truly equal.

Mansfield became more deeply involved in the 1972 election campaign than most people knew. According to his memoirs, McGovern first asked Edward Kennedy and then Senator Gaylord Nelson of Wisconsin to be his vice-presidential nominee, and after both declined, he turned to Thomas Eagleton of Missouri. Mansfield at first told McGovern that he could not have made a better choice than Eagleton. The revelation of Eagleton's earlier severe depression and electric shock treatment caused him to be dropped from the ticket, and the McGovern campaign never recovered. When asked for his advice, Mansfield cautioned McGovern to keep Eagleton on the ticket. After McGovern decided to drop Eagleton, he asked Mansfield to be his running mate, explaining: "It seemed to me that the Senate Majority Leader would have been a reassuring choice after the divisive chaos of the preceding days." McGovern writes that Mansfield "said he would not even consider that. He told me that Lyndon Johnson had tried to persuade him to be his running mate in 1964, but that he had stoutly refused. Mike Mansfield . . . honestly preferred the Senate to the presidency," concluded McGovern.

In his memoirs, McGovern marvels that Mansfield never told the press about this offer. I interviewed Francis Valeo, a top aide who was with Mansfield for 30 years and who Mansfield himself said knew him better than anyone but his wife, Maureen. Valeo told me that he did not know about that vice-presidential offer. Mansfield did not talk about it at all, and until McGovern's memoirs were published, it was something that was generally unknown.

I found a fascinating note in Mansfield's papers that I believe was written by Thomas Eagleton. It puzzled me at first because it was dated 1974, and this episode occurred in 1972. After talking to Valeo, it occurred to me that it took Eagleton two years to discover that Mansfield had been offered the vice-presidential slot. It was a rather embittered note that said, "Congratulations! Joe Robinson ran for Veep with Al Smith. Senator Jim Reed of Missouri declined the Veep nomination in 1928, saying: 'I refuse to take a back seat on a hearse!'" Mansfield's papers were put together very quickly, but I still found them useful, especially that particular note.

Last week, the Senate Historical Office graciously sent their 900-page interview with Frank Valeo to me. It had been conducted in 1985 and early 1986 but had a ten-year moratorium placed on it. After reading that interview, I had to rethink my position. My focus was Vietnam and Mansfield, and while the issue of leadership seemed central, in truth it was not for Mansfield because he did not believe in using his leadership position to push his own agenda. Even though he potentially had great power in the Senate, both as leader and as the perceived expert on the Far East, he did not use that status to try to end the war. When he did speak out, he simply spoke as an individual.

One incident that got my attention when looking at the *Congressional Record* from 1953, Mansfield's first year in the Senate, was the high praise he paid to two Senate colleagues. One was Minority Leader Lyndon Johnson, who was clearly on his way to becoming a powerful entity. The other was John Kennedy, who was not a powerful entity in 1953. His remarks are rather funny in retrospect. Mansfield said that Kennedy was "one of the hardest working and most respected members of the Senate. While young in years, he is wise in experience, and he has given freely of his advice and counsel to many of his colleagues." In his statement praising Johnson, he said:

I have been not only pleased but flattered by the attention he has shown to those of us who have come to the Senate for the first time. He certainly has indicated to us a great wisdom, a wide field of knowledge, and a good deal of understanding. He has treated us as equals and he has asked us for our opinions, upon occasion.

That comment may have been a Freudian slip because Johnson did not ask people for their opinions very often. Likewise, Kennedy was well known for not being a hardworking senator. Mansfield admitted as much in an oral history interview in 1964 for the Kennedy Library. Both tributes seem like pandering, and I wondered why Mansfield chose those two men. Either he was lucky or he was prophetic because these two men brought him to more power than any senator from Montana has ever held. Montana is an unlikely state to produce a majority leader or a presidential candidate. More than luck was involved. I believe that he was prophetic. Frank Valeo made some comments that have helped me firm up that position.

First, Valeo talked about Mansfield's ambition and said that regarding foreign policy, Mansfield liked the spotlight just as much as any other senator. Mansfield liked to be covered by the press. He cultivated an image, a tight-lipped Gary Cooper persona, that was very effective and is still legendary. The man understood public relations. I do not know if that image would have been as helpful to him in running for the presidency, but it sold well in Montana.

Regarding Mansfield's acceptance of the whip position in 1956, Valeo said that while Mansfield took the position reluctantly, he took everything reluctantly. That point is important to remember. In speaking of Mansfield's acceptance of the majority leadership in 1960, Valeo speculated:

It is very, very difficult to discuss Mansfield's motives. Even I, who probably knew him as well as anyone around by the time he left—as a matter of fact, he said at one time, that I knew him probably as well as anybody will ever know him, except his wife. It is very hard to explain his motives. . . . You can either see him as a master Machiavellian or as a very honest, simple man who just did not really want anything that came his way. But a great

70

deal came his way. (Valeo, Senate Historical Office interview, pp. 159–60)

In discussing the 1964 vice-presidential trial balloon, Valeo said something that shocked me. Although Mansfield had rarely attended previous nomination conventions, he did go in 1964 and for the first time ever asked Frank to go with him. Valeo concluded, without Mansfield ever having told him so, that he was there to write an acceptance address if the vice-presidential nomination were offered. Valeo said that all Mansfield told him was to "listen and see if you hear anything interesting." Since he assumed that he was there to write the vice-presidential acceptance speech if it were offered, he began working on a rough draft, probably unbeknownst to Mansfield. Valeo said that Mansfield was ambivalent about not being offered the vice presidency:

> Again, he's a complex man, and there may have been a little bit of both in it. I mean, he was relieved on one hand, but probably, in my judgment, disappointed. He expected Johnson to perhaps name him. (Valeo, pp. 348–50)

At another point in the interview he suggested that Mansfield may have seriously thought about the vice presidency in 1964. In 1956, he was a long shot. In 1972 McGovern was a sinking ship, and Mansfield knew it. In 1964, however, the Democrats were convinced they could win against Goldwater. Mansfield may have seriously thought about being vice president.

Valeo also said in that interview:

> It's interesting, Mansfield always was on his guard against senators who were running for the presidency. He had an early warning system which told him apparently who they were. He had it on [Scoop] Jackson, he had it on [George] McGovern. He knew early in the game that McGovern was thinking of the presidency—probably even before McGovern knew it himself. He used to always treat them with a certain amount . . . [of] standoffishness. His interest was in Senate personalities and he didn't warm to people who were running for the presidency in

the Senate. It's either that, or he was thinking of running for the presidency himself. I don't really know for sure. (pp. 839-40)

From the interview, it sounds as though so many people in the Senate were positioning themselves for the vice-presidential or presidential bid that the Senate could barely function.

The popular belief that Mansfield was not interested in higher office probably will go down in history because the only contradiction is Valeo's interview. The possibility of seeking higher office was probably at the back of his mind, but he was not going to pursue it actively. I know that he told Lyndon Johnson he did not want the position, but he also knew that if Johnson pushed the point, the party's vice-presidential nomination would have been hard to refuse. Johnson was correct in that assessment.

Valeo described Representative Mansfield when he first met him in the late 1940s as "sort of a gangly figure; he was sort of rawboned. He looked like he'd been clothed at J. C. Penney's." I found that description endearing. Journalist Linda Ellerbee suggested on 17 September 1976 that Mansfield "combined the eloquence of Calvin Coolidge and Gary Cooper." The *New York Times* once called his delivery a "firm monotone" and considered him "colorless . . . the hue of his suit would depress an undertaker." Ted Kennedy once quipped that Mansfield's five favorite replies were "yep," "nope," "maybe," "could be," and "don't know." Still, Mansfield was known as the "fastest gun in the West" by the media because he gave answers so quickly on television panel shows that reporters sometimes ran out of questions before the programs ended. He once answered 76 questions when his questioners had only expected to ask 25 questions. Some aspects of that distant persona and succinct style of speech might have endeared him to voters, but he would have been a strange presidential candidate.

Nevertheless, he was certainly a fine statesman. Of the three dissertations on Mansfield, the one written by David Turner condemned him for his role in the Vietnam War. While I can understand that point, I do not agree with it. It is true that he helped to commit the United States to support South Vietnam in 1954, since he believed that Eisenhower was going to do so anyway. Mansfield helped persuade Eisenhower and Secretary of State John

Foster Dulles to support Vietnamese nationalist Ngo Dinh Diem, and I argue in my book that Diem was probably the right choice *if* the United States felt compelled to make a choice at all. By the time that Kennedy was in office, however, Mansfield was sending term-paper-length memos against escalation of the Vietnam War. He later implored Johnson and Nixon to try to end the war. From my perspective, his position on the Vietnam War was correct, except perhaps in 1954.

In conclusion, Mansfield was a great statesman, a fine politician, and a legend in Montana. He is to Montana what Robert La Follette is to Wisconsin or Hubert Humphrey is to Minnesota. He is revered as Montana's preeminent political figure.

NARRATOR: How do you interpret Mansfield's role as "godfather" to South Vietnamese President Ngo Dinh Diem?

MR. OLSON: I think that period is the most fascinating part of the United States' entry into Vietnam. Mansfield used his appointment to the Foreign Relations Committee, which he owed to Lyndon Johnson, to pay visits to Vietnam in 1953, 1954, and 1955. Mansfield and Kennedy were introduced to Diem in May 1953 by Justice William Douglas, who had previously been to Vietnam and had praised Diem more highly than was probably warranted. Lacking background knowledge, Mansfield asked no questions at that meeting, unlike Kennedy and Douglas. After that meeting he began studying Indochina in depth. In 1954 he met Diem again, and his favorable report probably paved the way for the Eisenhower administration to announce that future U.S. aid would be funneled directly to Diem instead of through France. One historian said that Mansfield's report became the "cornerstone" of the Eisenhower administration's support policy.

Mansfield was largely responsible for saving Diem in the spring of 1955. Eisenhower had sent General J. Lawton Collins as temporary U.S. ambassador to straighten out the situation, which was in pretty bad shape. Even though Mansfield and some in the State Department were supporting Diem, Collins wanted Diem replaced because he did not believe that Diem was viable. It was interesting that all of the State Department memos were given to

Mansfield. His dictated replies were cabled to Paris and then relayed to Saigon because there was no direct link from Washington to Saigon. Mansfield was credited by Joe Alsop with becoming the "deciding factor" in the Eisenhower administration's decision to stay with Diem. It is true that other people were involved, such as Colonel Edward Landsdale, a CIA operative in Saigon who proved crucial to Diem's winning his battle with two religious groups and a group of heavily armed gangsters. Nevertheless, Mansfield was quite influential in those early years. It is ironic that Secretary of State John Foster Dulles, who knew nothing about Southeast Asia, deferred to Mansfield, a first-term senator from a sparsely populated state and a member of the opposite party of the President. Author William Conrad Gibbons says that there were fewer than five American experts on that area at the time. The United States entered into that part of the world totally ignorant. Mansfield created the perception that he was an expert, and eventually he really became one, although he initially exaggerated his credentials. He had received a master's degree from the University of Montana, written his thesis on U.S.-Korean relations, and stayed at the University of Montana to teach Far Eastern history.

One of the interesting ways Mansfield created his persona was by simply not correcting errors that exaggerated his credentials. In the early 1940s President Roosevelt had sent Mansfield to China, and his trip report helped to establish his credentials. This reputation hurt him later when he ran for the Senate in 1952. Wisconsin's Senator Joe McCarthy went to Montana to campaign against Mansfield and sent Harvey Matusow as well who called Mansfield a Communist dupe. After the China trip, prominent journalist Drew Pearson wrote that Mansfield was one of the few Chinese-speaking members of Congress. Mansfield had spent time in the Marines in the Philippines after World War I and was sent to China for some 12 days during a warlord battle that was threatening the international community at Tientsin. He became fascinated with China, but he did not learn to speak Chinese. He did not speak any foreign languages and did not even take lessons in Japanese after he became U.S. ambassador in Tokyo.

Mansfield had a policy about never correcting mistakes made about him in the press, which can be a somewhat self-serving philosophy. In 1958, the *New York Times* referred to him as "one of the few Chinese-speaking members of Congress," so the press believed that he spoke Chinese, even though he did not.

Another fascinating fact about Mansfield is that the press loved him. He was very open and gave answers that were short but honest. He did not use a press secretary. Valeo and Mansfield were always in the office on Saturdays, and they would meet with anyone from the press. Furthermore, he was very supportive of the press. It was during the Kennedy administration that the credibility gap really began. The Kennedy administration lied to the press about the role of the United States in the coup that toppled Diem, as well as the military situation in South Vietnam. Majority Leader Mansfield chose a different tack. Mansfield once received a warm telegram from David Halberstam, Neil Sheehan, and other war correspondents who were not toeing the administration line, and they said they wished that they were voting residents of Montana. Because of the press's liking for Mansfield, reporters did not blame Mansfield for what he had said about Vietnam in 1953 and 1954. He had been the token Democrat, sent by Eisenhower to sign the Southeast Asia Treaty Organization (SEATO) agreement. When he later opposed the use of SEATO as justification for the war during the Johnson administration, Dean Rusk could not understand his decision. After Mansfield told Rusk that he had signed the agreement reluctantly, Rusk checked the *Congressional Record*. He wrote in his memoirs that there was no sign that Mansfield had been reluctant to sign the agreement, and Rusk was right. In fact, Mansfield praised SEATO from the Senate floor, although I still think that he was reluctant to agree to it. He worried about white nations imposing collective security arrangements on their former colonies. Mansfield also thought that not having India as a member would be a problem, and he was probably right. Yet the press never criticized Mansfield's earlier positions on Vietnam.

At the time of the Gulf of Tonkin incident, Mansfield clearly did lie. He was almost the only person to speak against the resolution in private, but in public he supported it. He and Fulbright quickly rammed it through Congress. I asked Mansfield how he could account for his different statements in public and private, and he replied that he did not remember the differences at that time.

The strategy of publicly supporting the President while criticizing him in private was also Fulbright's strategy for a while. Both men decided that if they could be heard in private, maybe they would eventually be able to influence Johnson. Mansfield wrote memos recommending that the United States hold on to coastal enclaves and go to the bargaining table without additional escalation. His public position was not a total turnaround. Mansfield would go as far as he could to support Johnson. He even did the same with Richard Nixon for a long time. Before Nixon made his silent majority speech in November 1969, Mansfield wrote a long epistle to Nixon, which basically said that the Democrats would take the blame for the war as long as U.S. forces withdrew promptly. Nixon at that time did not think he could withdraw forces and ignored Mansfield's offer.

QUESTION: Did Mansfield persuade Kennedy to get out of Vietnam?

MR. OLSON: Mansfield does not claim credit for that decision, but he thinks that Kennedy would have kept U.S. troops out of the conflict. Kennedy aide Kenneth O'Donnell's memoirs, titled *"Johnny, We Hardly Knew Ye;" Memoirs of John Fitzgerald Kennedy* (1972), contains an account of a meeting with Mansfield in which Kennedy said that the United States had to leave. Mansfield's 1962 report is considered rather famous; it countered all of the administration reports that said the United States was gradually winning. In the spring of 1963 Kennedy said that the United States had to get out of Vietnam, but not until after the 1964 election because a McCarthyite red scare could occur. It is unclear from O'Donnell's account what was said when Mansfield was at the meeting and what was said after he left.

Mansfield produced a large quantity of correspondence about Vietnam. In three different letters he denied O'Donnell's account and said that Kennedy did understand that he could not withdraw the 16,000 U.S. troops overnight, but that this move would have to be done gradually. Nothing was said in connection with the 1964 election, however. Mansfield said he had no idea what O'Donnell and Kennedy discussed after he left.

Author John Newman has written a book, *JFK and Vietnam: Deception, Intrigue, and the Struggle for Power* (1992), in which he argues that Kennedy had a clear intention of getting out of Vietnam but was forced to be duplicitous because the "powers that be" did not want to get out of Vietnam. I do not agree with that assessment. One of Kennedy's journalist friends said that Kennedy was uncertain about what to do about the Vietnam situation, which is a more accurate statement. Kennedy considered Mansfield's advice and probably told Mansfield and Wayne Morse what they wanted to hear—that he was not going to get more deeply involved. Certainly, the steps he took were very hawkish, however. His administration allowed Diem to be overthrown, even though they were confused about this decision. Once the United States allowed Diem to be eliminated, there was a certain moral obligation to the new leaders who followed. Johnson was frustrated by the number of coups that followed. Westmoreland argued that the Diem coup was the big mistake because that event essentially committed the United States to the conflict.

QUESTION: Several people have written that Mansfield wanted to continue as ambassador to Japan even after some suggested that he be replaced. Is that depiction of the situation accurate?

MR. OLSON: Carter first offered him the ambassadorship to Mexico, which made sense because he had been a professor of the Far East and Latin America at the University of Montana. He turned down the ambassadorship in Mexico, writing to Carter that the air pollution in Mexico City would harm his wife Maureen, who was not well in 1976. A great deal of pressure was placed on Carter to find a post for Mansfield. Mansfield wanted China, but labor leader Leonard Woodcock became ambassador to China. The Japan ambassadorship was offered to Mansfield next. According to one report Mansfield asked Gerald Ford to intervene with Ronald Reagan in 1980 so that he could keep the post in Japan; Ford did so, and Mansfield was kept in that post. Both Jimmy Carter and Ronald Reagan have stated independently that keeping Mansfield in Japan was the only thing on which the two men ever agreed. Mansfield was considered somewhat pro-Japanese, at least in the early 1980s. He was quoted in business magazine articles as always saying that Americans have to look at the situation from the Japanese point of view as well, that the fault for problems between the two countries did not rest solely with the Japanese. That attitude was frustrating to some people. I found one article that praised current Ambassador Walter Mondale while it at least indirectly criticized Mansfield's term of service in Japan. In the Montana press, of course, only good things were said about Mansfield.

QUESTION: What was Mansfield's feeling on whether Cambodian Prince Norodom Sihanouk should be supported or released?

MR. OLSON: Mansfield was the first public figure to visit Sihanouk and helped reestablish relations with his government before Nixon sent troops into Cambodia in May 1970. Mansfield was one of the few people to speak out in favor of Sihanouk's decision to renounce American aid after the Diem assassination. They were on very close terms. Several members of the Cambodian Lon Nol government tried to urge Mansfield to intercede with Sihanouk on their behalf while he was visiting China, but Mansfield did not do so for reasons unknown. He had planned on interceding once and suggested to Kissinger that he would be an intermediary if asked, but Kissinger did not ask. Years later, Sihanouk visited Mansfield in Japan twice. Mansfield told me that they talked about finding a compromise political settlement in Cambodia—the one that Sihanouk now has.

Fulbright once said that Mansfield had met more heads of state than anyone he ever knew. Mansfield had those relationships with Sihanouk, Diem, and Prince Souvanna Phouma in Laos. He also visited Burma often and had a close relationship with Philippine president Ferdinand Marcos. Marcos gave Mansfield a beautiful desk. U.S. law prohibited Mansfield from keeping it personally, so he donated it to the Mansfield Library.

QUESTION: Did Frank Valeo and Mansfield remain close after Mansfield left the Senate?

MR. OLSON: Mansfield did not have close friends. He and Francis Valeo traveled the world together, but they apparently had little contact after they both left the Senate in January 1977. Valeo left the Senate when Mansfield did because the secretary of the Senate is a political position that is usually appointed by the majority leader.

QUESTION: Did the fact that Mansfield was Catholic have anything to do with his rise in politics or the decisions he made? It must have affected his eligibility on the presidential ticket.

MR. OLSON: He was a Catholic. One of the Johnson cronies said that his relationship with Kennedy was similar to the Texas gang in that they shared a common outlook. This factor had an influence because Mansfield grew up in an era when Catholics were discriminated against.

Until 1990 Montana had two congressional districts, and Mansfield ran in the western one. Montana is unique in that the western part was settled before the eastern section. Most Catholics in Montana live in the western part, so being Catholic was probably not a big drawback for him. Mansfield was denied high school teaching jobs for which he had applied in two small communities, and he thought that it was because he was Catholic. In that sense, being a Catholic did affect him. Valeo talks about the social consciousness of being Catholic, and some argue that there is a worldview or a certain set of values that come from that religious background. In 1952 when he ran for the Senate, another Catholic was seeking the eastern House seat, and many nasty telephone calls were made about not sending another Catholic to Washington.

Mansfield denied that being Catholic had anything to do with his support of Diem, but I think it did. Vietnam was such an oddity. The early military people there referred to Laos as the Land of Oz, and Vietnam was not much different. Warlords with private armies and religious sects—such as the Cao Dai, which had its own pope and female cardinals—were in those countries. The fact that Vietnam had a minority Catholic population and that Diem was a devout Catholic clearly had a great deal to do with Mansfield's position on Vietnam. William Douglas, John Kennedy, and especially his father, Joe Kennedy, were among the many Catholics pushing to have a Catholic in control of a country that was not more than 9 percent Catholic. The situation did create problems.

QUESTION: In view of Mansfield's personality, how did he make the switch from academic life to politics? I would not have thought this change to be a natural progression.

MR. OLSON: According to the story that Mansfield has cultivated, which is probably true, his interest in politics began in 1936. As Valeo also implies, the main decisions were made by Maureen.

Mansfield enlisted in the Navy toward the end of World War I and got to see Ireland from the ship, although he never set foot there. He was looking for adventure. He enlisted in the Navy at the age of 14 by lying about his age, and he then enlisted in the Army. Because he was from Montana, the base commander put him in charge of caring for his daughter's horse. He did not like that job, so he joined the Marines and went to the Philippines. He was always a big fan of the Marines after that experience. Following his stint in the Marines, he returned to Montana and worked in the mines.

Mansfield made some nice political connections while in Montana. At various times he lived in Butte, Great Falls, and Missoula, the three major cities in that district. He joined the union while working in the mines and had also been secretary of the faculty union of the University of Montana during his teaching career. Therefore, he had a great deal of labor support, unlike the stereotypical academic eggheads who have difficulty relating to the masses. Service as a private in three different branches gives one military credentials. Maureen argued that he was likeable and had had vast experience, so he should therefore run for office.

He ran in 1940, but finished third in a four-person Democratic race. Jeannette Rankin came out of retirement to run as a Republican and won. Mansfield then campaigned for the next two years, knowing that Rankin was not reelectable after her vote against entry into World War II. He won in 1942 with the help of his students.

The only close race he ever had was the 1952 Senate race against an ineffective incumbent Republican.

NARRATOR: Could he have done anything about the breakdown of consensus between the Republicans and Democrats after Vietnam? Does the fact that he got along with Republicans in the Senate suggest something about what he might have done if he had been president?

MR. OLSON: A case can be made that Mansfield's leadership style was absolutely central to passage of the Civil Rights Act of 1964. The fact that Republicans trusted him made it possible to carry out a long-term strategy of bringing Everett Dirksen around. Mansfield had all of the meetings in Dirksen's office, but when they posed for pictures afterward, he did not show up. He even tried to persuade *Time* magazine not to put his picture on the cover after the Civil Rights Act was passed. All of these incidents contribute to the idea that he did not have an ego. He did not mention the Civil Rights Act as one of his great accomplishments, and I do not think he considers himself responsible for it.

Mansfield told me that he considered himself a failure on the issue of Vietnam. Nevertheless, I tend to think that those years of trying to convert his colleagues played a key role. The Senate forced the end of the war, and Mansfield certainly had something to do with that situation. At the time of his retirement, he considered the passage of CIA oversight legislation as one of his major achievements. He had fought for that legislation since the 1950s. He convinced North Carolina Senator Sam Ervin to chair the Watergate Committee, and he thought that he had made a good choice, an opinion with which I agree. He fought for passage of the amendment allowing 18 year olds the right to vote, although he admitted that the results did not seem effective in the short term.

Frank Valeo said that the 1964 Civil Rights Act and Mansfield's efforts to persuade colleagues on Vietnam policy were his two most significant accomplishments. I think Valeo is right. I do not share Mansfield's pessimistic self-assessment. Even though his success cannot be measured, he did help bring the Senate around to his way of thinking in opposing the Vietnam War.

QUESTION: Is there any particular reason for why Senator Mansfield had such widespread acceptance and trustworthiness?

MR. OLSON: It was by design. I do not mean that he was dishonest about who he was, but rather that he deliberately tried to establish a certain persona. Studies indicate that expertise and trustworthiness are the two big factors in credibility, and certainly he was considered to have both. Dynamism is a third factor, and I suspect that he did not have much dynamism. The fact that he was perceived to be nonpartisan certainly helped him to gain the confidence of Republicans.

His first two or three years as majority leader were rocky. Frank Valeo says that Connecticut Senator Thomas Dodd was drunk when he made the attack on Mansfield in the Senate, and Morse criticized Mansfield at another time. Many Democrats said that Mansfield did not lead as he should have. From my reading, all of those criticisms ended after the passage of the Civil Rights Act. People were afraid that the courts would end up issuing rulings to define the scope of civil rights because the Senate would never be able to get enough votes for cloture to pass the necessary legislation. Senators thought so well of themselves after 1964 and the passing of the Great Society legislation in 1965 that Mansfield's stature rose along with that of the institution. Many senators still speak of Mansfield with reverence, including William Proxmire, who thought Mansfield was the ideal kind of leader.

In summary, Mansfield's success was not due to any single factor. Probably the most important of many factors was simply the fact that the press liked him and that he was a likable man.

NARRATOR: We thank Gregory Olson for providing a new, interesting perspective on Senator Mike Mansfield.

CHAPTER FIVE

J. William Fulbright*

RANDALL BENNETT WOODS

NARRATOR: Randall Bennett Woods has done significant research and writing on Senator J. William Fulbright. Mr. Woods is the John A. Cooper Professor of Diplomatic History and Distinguished Professor at the University of Arkansas. His course, "The United States in Vietnam, 1945-1976," is listed as the best course at the University of Arkansas in Lisa Birnbaum's *Guide to U.S. Colleges and Universities* (1992).

Professor Woods has published several books, including *The Roosevelt Foreign Policy Establishment and the Good Neighbor: Argentina and the United States, 1941-1945* (1979); *A Black Odyssey: John Lewis Waller and the Promise of American Life, 1878-1900* (1981); *A Changing of the Guard: Anglo-American Relations, 1941-1946* (1990); *The Dawning of the Cold War: America's Quest for Order, 1945-1950* (1991); *J. William Fulbright: A Biography* (1995); and *Interpreting America* (with William B. Gatewood, two volumes forthcoming, 1996-1997). He will talk about Senator Fulbright.

MR. WOODS: I will begin my presentation with some background about Senator Fulbright and then relate it to his politics.

Presented in a Forum at the Miller Center of Public Affairs on 1 March 1996.

Mr. Fulbright's father was a banker and businessman. The Fulbrights lived in Fayetteville, Arkansas, which is in the northwest part of the state and is the site of the University of Arkansas. They arrived in 1905 and became a major power in the town. There was a good bit of resentment toward the Fulbrights even as late as 1971 when I arrived in Fayetteville because they controlled most of the real estate, the principal business, and the newspaper. It was a Fulbright family town.

The northwestern part of the state was sympathetic to the Union during the Civil War. Blacks comprised less than 2 percent of the population in that area. It was very homogenous, which was very atypical of the South and different from both the Delta and the rest of Arkansas. Because Mr. Fulbright grew up in that environment, he did not have much contact with the ethnic diversity and poverty that characterized the eastern part of the state and the South in general. He was also very much a part of the provincial aristocracy. His parents were both college graduates. His mother edited the town paper and was politically active, and they often had college professors and politicians as guests in his home. He created an image of himself as a hayseed bumpkin from Arkansas and a country boy come to Washington, but his early life was not as culturally deprived as he liked people to believe. That depiction simply was not true.

Fulbright was educated entirely at the University of Arkansas, from the time he entered an experimental grammar school run by the College of Education until he graduated from college. The grammar school and high school were quite avant-garde, rooted in the philosophy and teaching methods of John Dewey. He and his classmates, for example, read such radical writers as Charles Beard. It was truly an unusual educational experience for a young man from Arkansas to have in those years. He was active in campus politics as an undergraduate and was an Arkansas Razorback football star, which put him in good stead later when people accused him of being a Communist. It proved impossible for Arkansans to believe that a Razorback could actually be a Communist. He did not realize that being an athlete would later become a political credential that served him well.

In 1925 one of Fulbright's professors told him about the Rhodes Scholarship competition that was then underway and persuaded him to enter it. His mother's political influence greatly facilitated his being selected for this program. He was a good student, but not a great one. His mother was close friends with John Futrall, the president of the University of Arkansas and chairman of the selection committee. Fulbright was always quite frank in acknowledging that his mother's influence was decisive in his obtaining the scholarship.

Fulbright's time at Oxford changed him dramatically, though he was not quite as out of place as one might think. The Fulbrights had friends who traveled in Europe, including some who lived in London and Oxford at the time, so it was not quite the alien experience he later portrayed it to be. His mother was a raving Anglophile, and her son going to Oxford was the high point of her life. He reveled in the experience, particularly the opportunity to travel the Continent. His tutor was a Scotsman named Ronald MacCallum who was active in the Liberal Party. Fulbright's education emphasized the values of English liberalism: equality of opportunity, republicanism, individual responsibility, and free trade. MacCallum, an avid Wilsonian, later wrote a book in 1944 defending collective security and appealing to the Western world to embrace internationalism.

Fulbright graduated in 1929 and decided to spend a year on the Continent. Like many young people, he went to Vienna to experience the cafe life there, and he met a remarkable Hungarian-American man named Mike Fodor. Fodor, then a correspondent for the *Manchester Guardian* and the *New York Evening Post*, was friends with Dorothy Thompson and had extensive political contacts in eastern and southeastern Europe. For a year he and Fulbright toured the Balkans together, and Fulbright was able to meet with heads of state, foreign ministers, and other important people. It was a remarkable political education for him. He could have become a foreign correspondent, and indeed, he later said he would have done so if he had not become ill. Instead, he returned home to Fayetteville and went into the family business.

While on a business trip to Washington in 1930, he met his future wife, Elizabeth Williams of Philadelphia. To be near her, he entered George Washington University Law School, and they were married in 1932. He received a law degree from GWU and worked for the Justice Department for a brief period before returning to Arkansas in 1936 to help his mother with the family business. There he began to teach part-time at the law school, and he settled down and became a kind of country squire. His mother had other ideas and ambitions for him, however. When John Futrall was suddenly killed in 1939, she used her influence to have her son appointed as the new president of the University of Arkansas. He was then the youngest university president in the United States, and even though he was unqualified, he did a respectable job for two brief years. In 1941 an Arkansas politician and political enemy of the Fulbrights named Homer Adkins was elected governor, and he quickly fired the president of the U of A.

In an abrupt career transition, Fulbright then ran for Congress in 1942 and won. He came to national attention in 1943 when he co-sponsored the Fulbright Resolution, which placed Congress on record as favoring membership in a postwar collective security organization. (That organization later became known as the United Nations.) It was then that he first came to the attention of the Roosevelt White House and liberal internationalists.

In 1944 he ran successfully for the Senate, defeating Homer Adkins, the same race-baiting, reactionary governor who had fired him from the post of president of the University of Arkansas. It was a bitter campaign, the hardest he would fight until 1974 when he lost to Dale Bumpers. After the election, Fulbright huddled with his assistants and planned his future. They recognized that there were basically two ways to stay in Congress. The first option was to attend to the needs of one's constituents, to hew quite closely to the economic interests of the state. The other was to make a splash on the national-international scene and become what he called a national senator. Fulbright opted for the latter course, since he felt he had some expertise in the area of foreign affairs. That goal was difficult to achieve, however. He did not get on the Senate Foreign Relations Committee until 1949.

In 1946, Fulbright sponsored legislation creating the Fulbright Exchange Program. He was appalled at Harry Truman and Ed Stettinius and believed that the country was being run by under-qualified, undereducated boobs. The Fulbright Exchange Program was designed to develop an educated, culturally aware, international intelligentsia in response to his perception of the void at the top. The program became his passion. He was not by nature a passionate man, and he valued rationality above all else, but he could become quite irrational in defense of the program. He would do anything and everything to defend and promote it. His enemies were aware of that fact, and in future years when they wanted to punish him, they did so by gutting the program. In 1967, for example, Lyndon Baines Johnson cut the program in half. Fulbright thought the exchange program was his most lasting contribution to the nation.

Fulbright was very much a conventional internationalist in the late 1940s. He supported the Marshall Plan and the Truman Doctrine. He was an Anglophile and an Atlanticist much like Dean Acheson. He viewed Stalinism as a threat to Western civilization and therefore supported measures designed to contain the forces of international communism.

His anticommunism, however, had limits. He disapproved of the trend in American foreign policy characterized by the globalization of containment, called for by NSC-68, a top-secret document unknown to him at the time. Like George Kennan, he believed that America's resources were limited and that its response to the threat of Communist expansion ought to be limited to only those areas of vital interest to the nation. He did not believe that the United States, as Tom Patterson put it, "could combat communism on every front."

He and Kennan were not friends—Fulbright did not have many friends. He did have a number of intellectual acquaintances and associates, however. He read Kennan's writings and was a great admirer of him from the early 1950s onward. He was friends with Walter Lippmann, both intellectually and socially. They remained associated for much of Fulbright's political life and found each other quite useful. They conferred and developed policy positions that Lippmann would tout in his editorial column and Fulbright would advance in the Senate.

Fulbright came to national attention and attracted the support of liberals when he confronted Senator Joseph McCarthy, who had attacked Fulbright's exchange program. They had violent debates during a series of hearings, and in February 1954 Fulbright was the only senator to vote against appropriating funds for McCarthy's Subcommittee on Investigations of the Senate Government Operations Committee. Fulbright was very active in the movement to censure McCarthy.

During this same period, Fulbright alarmed his liberal supporters by voting against various civil rights measures. He had joined a filibuster against the Fair Employment Practices Committee in 1946, and he signed the Southern Manifesto in 1956. He voted against every civil rights act that came before Congress until 1970. My book has raised some controversy on this point, but his position on race in my opinion has gotten more attention than it probably deserves. I think his role in influencing American foreign policy in Vietnam was more important than his role in race relations. On the other hand, one cannot understand Fulbright's position on Vietnam without understanding his views on race. As Fulbright's career developed, his reputation within the liberal community in the United States remained ambiguous; he was a paradox. His supporters dismissed his segregationist record on the grounds of political expediency, arguing that because Arkansas is a southern, reactionary state he had to vote in this way to stay in office. That assessment was probably correct during the 1950s. By 1963 or 1964, though, Arkansas had 100,000 black voters, and his advisers were actually telling him that he needed to reverse his stand and support civil rights measures. Nevertheless, he was unable or unwilling to do so until 1970.

As one might expect, Fulbright was disdainful of the Eisen-hower administration. He thought that John Foster Dulles was a religious fanatic, a "narrow-minded true believer," as he put it. He also thought that Eisenhower was just what he seemed to be at the time—a superficial, golf-playing, undereducated military man whom history had accidentally elevated to the presidency. He was very much a part of the early Democratic assault on Eisenhower's persona that was led by men like Arthur Schlesinger and John Kenneth Galbraith. They attacked Eisenhower for dumbing down America, creating a climate of anti-intellectualism, and emphasizing business and material things. In later years, however, he came to have much more respect and appreciation for Eisenhower.

Fulbright served as chairman of the Senate Foreign Relations Committee from 1959 until 1974, the longest reigning chairmanship in American history. Journalists who covered Fulbright when he chaired the committee remembered those years with fondness because back then one could speak of the Senate Foreign Relations Committee as an institution.

Fulbright was a master at creating and maintaining a legislative majority. Until at least 1970 he had a good relationship with the Republican minority. They might have disagreed with him, but they felt that he treated them fairly and was not blindly partisan. In part, this reputation stemmed from the fact that many of his best friends were Republicans. He was very much an eastern establishment figure. When he left Arkansas in 1950, he essentially left for good. His world became the Washington-New York-Boston corridor. His friends lived there; he traveled there; it was his world.

In 1959 he met Nikita Khrushchev for the first time and was deeply impressed with him. Afterward, Fulbright believed that peaceful coexistence and detente with the Soviet Union were real possibilities. His commitment was to a low-level, passive version of containment that would maintain the status quo until communism should collapse of its own internal contradictions. He was delighted with Jack Kennedy's election, even though he had spoken quite disparagingly of him when Kennedy was still a senator. Fulbright initially regarded Kennedy as a playboy who never came to the Senate Foreign Relations Committee meetings. In 1960, however, Fulbright joined the liberal Democrats' conversion to Kennedy, believing that he was bright, enlightened in his views on foreign affairs, nonideological, and committed to containing but not confronting communism. He also approved of the people whom Kennedy attracted, such as George Ball and Kenneth Galbraith.

Notwithstanding what he later said, Fulbright hoped to be appointed secretary of state, and I think Kennedy did consider him seriously for that position. Arthur Schlesinger, in *A Thousand Days: John F. Kennedy in the White House* (1965), argues that he did. I think on an intellectual level, Kennedy found Fulbright's ideas congenial and thought that he would be an interesting person with whom to work. It quickly became apparent, however, that his appointment was politically impossible. The NAACP, various Zionist organizations, representatives of the AFL-CIO, and others lobbied directly against his appointment.

There is an irony here. Civil rights activists such as Andrew Young and Julian Bond were making an argument to Kennedy that appointing a segregationist would be disastrous for U.S. relations with developing nations. They felt that it would handicap the United States in its ability to combat communism in the developing world. This argument was an ironic one to make against the man who had authored the largest student exchange program in the history of the world and who had stood for cultural understanding and close international relations. Fulbright's life was filled with such ironies. I think he was disappointed but also deeply grateful that the Kennedys went out of their way to make him feel that he had been seriously considered. Fulbright was closely involved with Kennedy's foreign policy team and was a leading advocate of the liberal internationalism that characterized the Kennedy years.

Fulbright welcomed what he believed to be a new emphasis on combating communism through nonmilitaristic methods such as foreign aid, educational exchange, and alignment of the United States with nationalist movements in developing countries. He preferred this nonideological, pragmatic approach to the Cold War, which emphasized culture and economics rather than arms. From 1959 through 1961 the radical right staged a comeback in this country, symbolized by the founding of the John Birch Society, and Fulbright engaged them in a kind of intellectual and political combat. The radical right constrained Kennedy, which Fulbright realized to a limited extent. He opposed the Bay of Pigs operation, and during the Cuban Missile Crisis he feared that the Kennedy administration was being co-opted by the radical right. Once that crisis passed and Soviet-American relations began to improve, Fulbright relaxed.

He was a great supporter of the Nuclear Test Ban Treaty and looked forward to the second Kennedy administration with a great deal of anticipation. Nevertheless, Fulbright was not terribly disturbed by Lyndon Johnson taking Kennedy's place after the assassination. Fulbright had dealt with Lyndon Johnson for years.

Randall Bennett Woods

He thought that Johnson perhaps was too interested in action and form and not enough in substance, but he believed that Johnson, like Kennedy, was a pragmatic Cold Warrior, a domestic liberal and an eminently effective and energetic man. Moreover, Johnson cultivated Fulbright quite effectively and quite deliberately in 1963 and 1964.

Mr. Fulbright sponsored the Gulf of Tonkin Resolution because he believed that it was necessary to help President Johnson defeat Barry Goldwater in 1964. Johnson told Fulbright that he was being attacked for being soft on communism and needed to take action in Vietnam for domestic political reasons. It was in that context that Fulbright guided the resolution through Congress, believing that it authorized only short-term, specific responses to North Vietnamese attacks on American personnel. He later claimed that he had received assurances that it would not lead to a wider war.

Fulbright expected to be Dean Rusk's replacement and was deeply disappointed and angry that Johnson did not consider him for secretary of state in 1964. Johnson did not even make a pro forma gesture of considering him, and I think Fulbright was deeply offended. Fulbright felt increasingly shunned and neglected, but he did not break with Johnson over Vietnam until 1965.

The issue that led Fulbright to break with Johnson was the Dominican intervention in the summer of 1965, when the United States landed more than 20,000 troops in the Dominican Republic, ostensibly to prevent a Castroite takeover there. Fulbright and his chief of staff, Carl Marcy, had information to the effect that there were probably only 12 Marxist-Leninists on the entire island. They believed that the whole operation was designed to prevent Juan Bosch from returning to the Dominican Republic. Bosch was leftist, but not a Communist, and hardly "Castro-like." Johnson went to great lengths to defend the Dominican intervention, claiming that many innocent people had been beheaded, blood was flowing in the streets, the Communists were ready to invade, and so forth.

Fulbright decided that he had to challenge the administration. He believed that Johnson was bending over backward to appease the radical right to such a degree that his foreign policy was being taken over by hard-line anti-Communists. The Senate Foreign

91

Relations Committee held hearings on the Dominican Republic, and in September 1965, Fulbright delivered a fiery speech denouncing the American intervention. That incident marked the end of the relationship between the two men. According to McGeorge Bundy, Robert McNamara, and others close to Johnson, the President's attitude was that one was either on his team or not on his team. He kept Rusk because, as he said, "Dean Rusk is as loyal as a beagle." Mr. Fulbright was not.

In the wake of the Dominican Republic intervention, Fulbright and the staff of the Senate Foreign Relations Committee began to look more deeply at the situation in Vietnam. During the suspension of U.S. bombing from Christmas 1965 through early 1966, Fulbright talked with the White House on numerous occasions and argued that the war in Vietnam was basically a civil war. On one side was a corrupt, pro-Western regime in Saigon that had been supported by the French and was now being supported by the Americans, and on the other side was a nationalist movement consisting of the Democratic Republic of Vietnam and the National Liberation Front. Fulbright got nowhere with that argument. When the administration resumed the bombing of Vietnam on 31 January 1966, Fulbright blasted the Johnson administration on national television for plunging the United States into a full-scale war against a fifth-rate military power halfway around the world that had no bearing on U.S. vital interests.

The following month the Senate Foreign Relations Committee held televised hearings featuring General James Gavin, George Kennan, and others who questioned the wisdom of America's presence in Vietnam. Those hearings escalated the conflict between the committee and the White House, particularly the personal conflict between Johnson and Fulbright. The private war between these two men became all the more bitter because they had spent most of their political lives associating with each other—they came not only from the same political party but from the same wing of the party. It was a kind of civil war and all the bloodier for it. Throughout 1966 and 1967 Fulbright dedicated himself and the Senate Foreign Relations Committee to destroying the consensus that Kennedy and Johnson had built in support of the war in Vietnam.

In 1967 *The Arrogance of Power* was published. It sold 400,000 copies over the next four years and made the top-25 list of nonfiction books. The book created a reputation for Fulbright that went far beyond his being the author of the Fulbright Exchange Program. Foreigners came to see him as an enlightened, educated, restrained man who could appreciate other cultures. They contrasted him with their image—right or wrong—of Lyndon Johnson, whom they regarded as a provincial reactionary and cultural imperialist who was ready to plunge the United States into armed adventure against perceived Communist threats everywhere in the world. Indeed, Fulbright had a better reputation abroad than domestically.

During 1967 and early 1968, Fulbright faulted Lyndon Johnson, the radical right, conservative political opportunists, anti-Communist ideologues, and the military industrial complex for the United States' imperial foreign policy in Vietnam and elsewhere. By the time Johnson left the White House in January 1969, however, Fulbright had come to see that it was the very same internationalism that he had espoused in the late 1940s that was responsible for U.S. involvement in Vietnam. The notion of a monolithic Communist threat, the domino theory, and the Munich analogy had all been used to justify the Marshall Plan and the Truman Doctrine, and Fulbright had espoused and believed in them. As a result, his ongoing opposition to U.S. foreign policy had kind of an edge to it because in critiquing the policy, he was critiquing himself. He felt a sense of responsibility and, I think, guilt for American failures.

Fulbright's relations with the Nixon administration were odd. He was appalled by Richard Nixon but enthralled by Henry Kissinger, who manipulated Fulbright as skillfully as he manipulated anyone that he encountered. Kissinger convinced Fulbright that he, Kissinger, represented the forces of enlightenment, reason, and restraint within the Nixon administration and that he was fighting tooth and nail to combat the forces of parochialism, xenophobia, imperialism, and racism. (Pat Buchanan was always cited as representative of the other group in the White House.) Fulbright thus supported Kissinger throughout the Nixon administration. He was obviously impressed by the opening to China and the easing of tensions with the Soviet Union, and he believed that Kissinger was committed to detente and peaceful coexistence. Fulbright and Kissinger also were in agreement on the situation in the Middle East. In 1970 Fulbright advocated a "land for peace" settlement, to be accompanied by an American guarantee of Israeli boundaries.

In 1967 he had introduced the National Commitments Resolution in Congress, which was passed in 1969. It was a simple statement by Congress that no administration could commit U.S. troops or military aid to any other nation without the express consent and approval of Congress. The resolution formed the intellectual and political basis for the Cooper-Church amendment, the McGovern-Hatfield amendment, and eventually the War Powers Act.

As these measures were being enacted in Congress, Fulbright stepped back and played a much less visible role. Fulbright tried to maintain a low profile because he believed that he had become so controversial during the Johnson administration—something of a lightning rod—that the cause would be better served with him out of the spotlight. It was Stuart Symington and the Symington Subcommittee on United States Security Agreements and Commitments Abroad that investigated the secret agreements made with Spain and Thailand, and that investigation exposed the war in Laos. These investigations, however, were really Fulbright's operation. Walter Pincus's mission to Laos and the Richard Moose-James Lowenstein trips to Southeast Asia, which brought to light the secret U.S. bombing of Cambodia, were all part of the Senate Foreign Relations Committee's broader effort to challenge the Nixon administration and the imperial presidency.

By 1970, Fulbright had done an about-face on the proper roles of the executive branch and Congress in foreign affairs. He began his career in Congress as a champion of executive dominance in foreign affairs, and by 1970 he was waging a campaign against the imperial presidency, asserting Congress's rightful prerogatives to influence foreign affairs. His opponents accused him of being inconsistent. He would reply that he was not a constitutional theorist and did not care about constitutional consistency. He had supported an executive-dominated foreign policy in the late 1940s because Congress represented the forces of isolationism and xenophobia while the executive branch approach was one of enlightened internationalism. By the late 1960s and early 1970s, he argued that the presidency had been captured by the radical right, anti-Communists, and the military-industrial complex, while Congress represented a more enlightened foreign policy. It was the only possible restraint on the imperial presidency.

Fulbright's segregationist views on race were intellectually crucial to his critique of the war in Vietnam. He argued that just as the civil rights court rulings and legislation of the 1950s and 1960s were an effort by the North to impose its will on the South in social and cultural matters, the war in Vietnam was a similar effort by one culture to impose its will on another, and indeed to obliterate that culture.

There is also a political connection between his views on race and the war in Vietnam. Working behind the scenes, Fulbright was able to create a broad consensus on behalf of the legislation leading up to the War Powers Act because his credentials as a narrow interpreter of the Constitution were clearly established. It was this constitutional conservatism that enabled him to bring both liberals such as George McGovern and Frank Church and conservatives such as John Stennis together to form this powerful congressional antiwar coalition.

The fact that he was an internationalist and a segregationalist is not only historically and intellectually curious but politically crucial. Had he not been a segregationist and had he supported those civil rights bills, I think he would have had a much more difficult time attracting conservatives to his antiwar cause. He may have been the only person in Congress who could have acted as that bridge.

QUESTION: Why didn't Fulbright become president?

MR. WOODS: I do not think he was emotionally and psychologically able to make that kind of commitment. Whereas Bill Clinton was willing to do anything and everything to become President of the United States, Fulbright did not like politics. He was a lousy politician. For instance, when he attended political events, instead of making the rounds and shaking everyone's hand, he would find some farmer and sit in a corner to discuss the price of soybeans. He had a reputation for being lazy because he often secluded himself in his office and read. He loved to read and believed that reading was important. Fulbright was a private man who recognized that he would have had to give up too much to run for president.

Another reason he would never have run for president is that he would have had to compromise his policy positions. For example, he would have had to support civil rights before he was ready to do so, or he would have had to modify his position on the Middle East situation. His advocacy of a land-for-peace deal seems quite reasonable now, but it was *not* considered reasonable in 1970. The Israeli government officially condemned him. Virtually every pro-Israeli, Zionist organization in this country publicly criticized him and tried to develop a strategy to defeat him. Fulbright just was not willing to court those special interest groups that he needed to court in order to win.

I do not think there was ever a chance that he would become president. I do not think he had a desire to become president. In a sense, nevertheless, his public life did revolve around the presidency in an attraction-repulsion cycle. His great task—the one he and Carl Marcy set for themselves in 1966—was to wrest influence over public opinion from an executive branch that had such advantages as access to the press and control over a vast bureaucracy. He and Marcy spent endless hours strategizing about how to accomplish that task. They finally turned the Senate Foreign Relations Committee into a type of alternative state department. Fulbright believed that Congress should exercise its prerogatives to the point of formulating an alternative foreign policy.

QUESTION: As a statesman who focused on national and international issues, how did Fulbright's constituents perceive him to be a benefit to them? Was it just his stand on civil rights, or were other factors involved?

MR. WOODS: It was much more than his stand on civil rights. When he first won a Senate seat in 1944, the man he defeated was Homer Adkins, a traditional Southern politician who had built his power base on state patronage positions. Fulbright understood that he could not challenge that political power network, so he and his strategists targeted another constituency: the University of Arkansas alumni. They lived in every community in Arkansas. They were teachers, lawyers, and other interested people who were eager to support a person who was educated, sophisticated, and cosmopolitan. They were attracted to him because he was a walking refutation of the image of their state as "Dogpatch." Also, these people were more likely to vote and be politically active.

Even people who disagreed with Fulbright came to be proud of him. People from Arkansas tend to hate Texans, all the more since Texans do not pay much attention to them. They have this strange hang-up with Texas. When Fulbright battled Johnson over Vietnam policy, they therefore thought it was wonderful. It satisfied some deep inner need that Arkansans had, even those who were hawkish on the war in Vietnam. They loved the role of the underdog. Many people were proud simply to be associated with him, even if they could not articulate why.

His position in state politics was not impregnable, however. Orval Faubus could have beaten him in the Senate race of 1962, according to the polls. Fulbright's people lined up the big money and persuaded the Kennedy administration to put pressure on Faubus not to run.

QUESTION: You said something to the effect that Fulbright believed there was a void in U.S. leadership in the foreign policy establishment. Do you there was such a void and is there still one?

MR. WOODS: The quality of the U.S. foreign policy establishment has varied greatly over the years. I think the consensus among historians is that Harry Truman's foreign affairs team did not work well. Jimmy Byrnes was not a good secretary of state, but George C. Marshall, Dean Acheson, Will Clayton, and George Kennan were thoughtful, bright, and energetic people. I think that Fulbright approved of the quality of those State Department people even though he sometimes may have differed with them over their ideas and policy objectives. While he did battle with various secretaries of state, he was a great supporter of the foreign service.

QUESTION: Why did he lose to Dale Bumpers?

MR. WOODS: By 1974, Israel had come to have a psychological attraction for the American people that was particularly poignant and dramatic in the wake of our nation's defeat in Vietnam. Fulbright's perceived opposition to Israel was the last straw for many people, and I am not talking about the Jewish vote, but Americans in general. One can also argue that in Dale Bumpers, liberals in Arkansas finally had a true liberal for whom they could vote. The alternatives prior to that time were so awful that liberals could not afford to vote against Fulbright.

Quite frankly, however, my opinion is that Fulbright did not want to win. His political aides found it impossible to get him to go back to Arkansas to campaign. Previously he would begin touring the state two years before the election, line up the big money, and drive out potential opponents. In 1974, his aides could not arouse his interest in campaigning until about ten months before the election.

Fulbright also did not like the new style of politics. He did not like makeup or 30-second sound bites. He once complained that they were trying to sell him like a bar of soap. If he had really been committed and campaigned actively as he had done before, he could have won. Bumpers said that if he had not entered the race, Faubus or someone like him would have won Fulbright's seat, and that statement is probably accurate.

NARRATOR: Mr. Woods has become one of the most distinguished professors at the University of Arkansas, and this interesting and informative discussion has demonstrated why. We thank our speaker very much for this presentation.

CHAPTER SIX

J. W. Fulbright*

LEE R. POWELL

NARRATOR: Lee Riley Powell earned a J.D. degree from the University of Virginia Law School with distinction. Currently, he is a member of the Clinton administration's NAFTA Advisory Committee. In fact, he met yesterday with representatives of Mexico and other countries to discuss issues and problems related to NAFTA. He is expected to join the administration.

Mr. Powell was previously a staff lawyer for U.S. District Judge Bill Wilson in Little Rock, Arkansas. In that capacity, he wrote drafts of court orders on such issues as racial and gender discrimination. Prior to that position he was communications director and legislative assistant to former Congressman Bill Alexander. He participated in Alexander's two successful campaigns as the communications director.

Earlier, he was a political reporter writing for audiences in Arkansas, Alabama, and Virginia. He won an Associated Press award for political writing and earned recognition for his biographical work, *J. William Fulbright and His Time* (1996). President Clinton wrote the foreword to this book, and Senator Fulbright, who passed away in February 1995, wrote the afterword.

Presented in a Forum at the Miller Center of Public Affairs on 1 May 1996.

The book has had near universally favorable reviews; Daniel Schorr, for example, called it a "towering biography of a towering figure." In addition to the above volume, Mr. Powell has written two additional books on Fulbright: *J. William Fulbright and America's Lost Crusade: Fulbright's Opposition to the Vietnam War* (1984) and *J. William Fulbright and America's Lost Crusade: Fulbright, the Cold War and the Vietnam War* (1988).

The series of forums the Miller Center is currently conducting was inspired by Dumas Malone, who asked almost every Miller Center speaker why great men are not elected president. We look forward to hearing Mr. Powell's views on whether Fulbright was a great man, and if so, why he never became president.

MR. POWELL: In the 1980s Senator Fulbright used to say that the United States should spend more time focusing on trade and economic development in Latin America and other Third World nations rather than chasing Communists around. Now that the Cold War is over, the U.S. government discusses NAFTA with Mexico's government officials rather than trying to persuade them to support the U.S. anti-Communist crusade abroad. Nevertheless, negotiations are more complicated in the post-Cold War era.

Among the most prominent senators of his time, Fulbright was virtually alone in not having any presidential ambitions. He had rejected the notion of a Fulbright presidential candidacy so emphatically and so many times that reporters stopped speculating about the possibility. One would have to review the early years of his career to find any discussion of Fulbright as a possible president.

In early 1945 the famous columnist Dorothy Thompson described Fulbright as a man of presidential timber who was destined for greatness. Then in the fall of 1945, Fulbright's first year in the Senate, he was the unanimous choice of a faculty committee at Columbia University to succeed Nicholas Murray Butler as president. Fulbright decided to turn down the offer, saying that he was already off to a good start in the powerful United States Senate. The man who eventually succeeded Butler was General Dwight Eisenhower, whose appointment has led to intriguing speculation as to what would have happened if Fulbright had accepted the Columbia presidency. He was clearly one of the rising young stars of the Democratic Party. He was a Rhodes scholar and an honors graduate of the George Washington Law School before working in the antitrust division of the Justice Department during the New Deal. Elected as a congressman at an early age, Fulbright sponsored a resolution that put the United States on record as supporting American participation in the United Nations organization. People often said that he might one day be president. Had he become president of Columbia University, he could have escaped from the "southern trap" of that era. To become elected senator or governor in a southern state, a politician had to make concessions to the right wing on the race issue. By making these concessions, he would necessarily antagonize the powerful northern liberal bloc. Thus, he recognized that the possibility of ever becoming president was very slim.

He received other accolades through the years. For example, many years later, Henry Kissinger would say, "Across the chasm of our policy differences, I greatly admired Senator Fulbright for his erudition, patriotism, and courage." This statement might be considered somewhat surprising in light of Fulbright's differences with President Nixon over the years. On the other hand, Kissinger had worked closely with Fulbright in initiating the détente policies with the Soviet Union and China, and Fulbright supported Kissinger's efforts to bring about a more evenhanded policy in the Middle East. Thus, it may not be so surprising that Kissinger would compliment Fulbright.

Probably the most surprising accolade for Fulbright came from Martin Luther King Jr., given the fact that Fulbright had a profoundly disappointing civil rights record. He had signed the notorious 1956 Southern Manifesto and voted against the major civil rights legislation. King wrote to him in late 1965 when Fulbright had just condemned President Johnson's intervention in the Dominican Republican and was becoming a critic of the Vietnam War. King said,

> In many respects, the destiny of our nation may rest largely in your hands. I know the tremendous price you pay for your outspoken critique of administration policy, and I write to you these few words simply as personal encouragement and to let

you know that there are many of us who admire and respect your role in our nation's international affairs.

When Fulbright passed away last year, the *New York Times* had a front-page obituary saying that a giant of the United States Senate was dead. Several years earlier, John Kenneth Galbraith had written, "Of all persons who for their foreign policy, I've wished might be president, Bill Fulbright stands first." Walter Lippmann once said that Fulbright was the bravest and wisest of counselors, and if there was any question of his being removed from the Senate, it would be a national calamity.

But if Lippmann, Galbraith, and others were highly complimentary of Fulbright as a great man, equal time should also be given to his critics. Harry Truman said he was an "over-educated Oxford SOB," and Lyndon Johnson said that he was a frustrated old woman because he had never found a president who would appoint him secretary of state. This statement was made in reference to the celebrated episode in 1960 when John F. Kennedy was on the verge of appointing Fulbright secretary of state but ultimately decided that he could not do so because of Fulbright's weak civil rights record. Robert Kennedy said that Fulbright had this "terrible impediment" of having signed the Southern Manifesto.

In studying Fulbright as a statesman who never became president, one question is, What were his prospects for becoming president? As I have already mentioned, they were slim and none. He lacked the necessary ambition, did not suffer fools gladly, and disdained the sort of backslapping campaigning that politicians must do to get elected. He also felt that his political power base in Arkansas was too small, and as late as 1991 he still thought that about Bill Clinton. He was proven wrong on that score, of course. In his day, the South voted for the Democratic Party, so it did not help for him to be from Arkansas. In Clinton's era, the South has been turning more Republican, so if the Democratic nominee comes from the South, he more or less steals electoral votes from the Republicans. The insuperable obstacle to Fulbright becoming president would have been his weak civil rights record. In addition, his constant challenges to the Cold War establishment antagonized many people like Dean Rusk and Dean Acheson, who opposed Fulbright as a possible secretary of state in 1960.

Even though others wished that Fulbright had been president, there is little or no evidence that Fulbright himself ever seriously considered it. It seems that one must think about becoming president a great deal if that person wants to do so, as exemplified by FDR and the two candidates this year. Clinton had been thinking about it ever since he elbowed his way to the front of the line and shook hands with President Kennedy when he was a Boys State delegate. Last year Bob Dole was asked by a reporter if he had thought about running again for president, and he replied that he had been thinking about it "a few minutes ago."

As for Fulbright, he made no move toward getting into politics at any level until he was in his 30s and suddenly found himself without a job after his abrupt dismissal as president of the University of Arkansas. Actually, there was a chain of events—one accident led to another—which culminated in Fulbright's ascension to the Senate. In 1939, the president of the University of Arkansas was killed in an automobile accident, and Fulbright's family, which was one of the wealthiest families in northwest Arkansas, used excellent connections with the governor to have Fulbright named as the new president of the university. As a Rhodes scholar and a brilliant young law professor, he also was highly qualified in his own right. His mother, Roberta Fulbright, was a prominent journalist in northwest Arkansas. She and other members of his family pushed him. Then when a former Ku Klux Klansman named Homer Adkins won the governor's office, a similar political coup led to Fulbright being fired as president of the University of Arkansas. Unemployment does concentrate the mind, and he decided to run for Congress in the following year, 1942. His first election campaign was a triumph, and two years later when that same Homer Adkins was running for the Senate, Fulbright decided to challenge him. He would have rather gone back home to Fayetteville than serve as a member of the House while Adkins was in the Senate. Once again, Fulbright won the election and gained national attention. So it is only a set of improbable events, along with the persuasion of friends and family, that projected him into the House of Representatives and later the Senate, where he would become one of the leading senators in American history.

One of the criticisms of Fulbright was, in the words of Dean Acheson, that he was too much of a disorganized dilettante to become a good president. Another criticism was that he was incapable of pushing a legislative program through Congress. It is true that throughout much of his career he played the role of a dissenter, and naturally someone in that role is not going to push many bills through Congress.

On the other hand, in the brief periods when he could cooperate with the executive branch, he had a good record of pushing bills through. In the Roosevelt administration, he was able to work with Cordell Hull and other administration officials in securing passage of the Fulbright Resolution, which declared support for U.S. participation in an international peacekeeping organization. During the Truman administration, he was able to get the Fulbright Act passed, thereby funding an international scholarship program by selling surplus U.S. property abroad. He also helped to pass the Nuclear Test Ban Treaty in the Kennedy administration, and he worked closely with Kissinger in getting SALT passed.

His crucial interest in diplomacy began in World War II. As a freshman member of Congress, he had sponsored the resolution advocating U.S. participation in a postwar international organization. Secretary of State Hull enthusiastically supported it, and Franklin Roosevelt thought it was a good idea. The Fulbright Resolution was skillfully handled, and his timing was perfect. In July 1943, a Gallup poll reported about 78 percent public approval for the resolution, and it passed easily in both houses of Congress.

As early as 1945, Fulbright's role as a dissenter is apparent. He was not the type to build coalitions as was FDR. In fact, he delivered several scathing criticisms of President Truman's foreign policy early in the new president's term, thereby demonstrating, as he would throughout his career, a talent for antagonizing the Cold War establishment. In his first speech in the Senate, he juxtaposed his bewilderment and dismay at the American fear of communism with his hope that the creation of the United Nations would bring about a new peaceful world order in the postwar era. He believed that the most destructive of all of the American xenophobias was the hatred of the Soviet Union and communism. In his view, the emotional superpatriots who played upon the popular fears and hatred of communism only revealed the weakness of their faith in the American system.

Despite his concerns over the damaging effects of extreme anticommunism, the prevailing theme of that first Senate address was resilient optimism. Only two years before, the House had implicitly embraced the principle of collective security by passing the Fulbright Resolution, and now the United States seemed willing to adopt the U.N. Charter. Seven months later, however, a combination of events changed Fulbright's thinking. The explosion of the atomic bomb at Hiroshima, the failure of the United States to accept U.N. supervision of its armaments, and the emerging hostility between America and Russia transformed his earlier optimism into a pessimism that essentially lasted for the remainder of his career. In his speeches in the autumn of 1945, he deplored the reality that instead of cooperating in the United Nations, the United States had already fallen into "quarreling with Russia like two big dogs chewing on a bone."

Fulbright did not go as far as did Henry Wallace in his critique of the Truman foreign policies. He felt that Stalin was aggressive and that the containment policies in Europe were wise. Nevertheless, he was skeptical of the universal anticommunism of the Truman Doctrine. Later in his career, this skepticism deepened, and the Cold Warrior establishment thus developed negative attitudes toward him. Rusk and Acheson would have blocked any Fulbright bid for the presidency, not to mention secretary of state.

One characteristic that Fulbright displayed throughout his career and that might have led him to become a great president (had he been elected through some quirk of fate) was courage. One of the most notable profiles of courage in modern American history was Fulbright's relentless opposition to the witch hunts of Joe McCarthy. In early 1954, there was an important test vote on appropriations for McCarthy's investigations. By that late date, many members of the Senate knew that McCarthy was a charlatan, yet they were afraid to confront him politically. The vote was 85 to 1 in McCarthy's favor. Fulbright cast the lone dissenting vote, which was typical of his role as a dissenter. His dissent obviously had no effect on the outcome of the vote, but it shocked some of the older members of the Senate into joining Fulbright in opposing McCarthy publicly. In fact, Senator Herbert Lehman stopped by Fulbright's office after the vote and apologized. After that point, Lehman became a vociferous public supporter of Fulbright in confronting McCarthy.

Shortly after this courageous vote against McCarthy, Fulbright rejected an FBI request for information on a State Department official. Fulbright knew that J. Edgar Hoover gave McCarthy access to his files, and that McCarthy used that information to smear people, including those who were not in any way Communist sympathizers. Fulbright said he would have given a favorable report on this official but refused to give McCarthy the opportunity to twist and distort the information in another of his character assassinations. A person who had enough courage to take on Joe McCarthy and J. Edgar Hoover at the same time had the kind of courage that would have been valuable in the White House.

Likewise, in the late 1950s, Fulbright was critical of John Foster Dulles. Again revealing his impressive courage, in 1961 Fulbright was the only member of the President's advisory team who advised him to cancel the Bay of Pigs invasion.

On the issue of Vietnam, Fulbright's record is more complicated, and on the subject of civil rights, it is pretty dismal. In the early 1960s, Fulbright was supportive of the Kennedy and Johnson policies in Vietnam, at least publicly. His strategy at that time was to advise the presidents in private to not intervene or escalate, but to publicly show support for them. This position raises the question of why Fulbright supported the Gulf of Tonkin Resolution in 1964. He certainly did not support escalation. In the spring of 1964 he sent a note to Secretary McNamara indicating his concern about the situation in Vietnam and asking if the United States should consider pulling out. In the midst of the Gulf of Tonkin debate, Fulbright said, "I personally feel it would be very unwise under any circumstances to put a large land army on the Asian continent." Why, then, did he support the resolution?

First, he was concerned about the threat of Barry Goldwater's candidacy, since Johnson was portraying himself as the man of peace who was not going to send American boys thousands of miles away from home to fight a war that Asian boys should be fighting for themselves. Goldwater had talked about using low-yield atomic bombs to defoliate the jungle trails in Vietnam. Fulbright thus regarded the Tonkin resolution as a political ploy, at least in part, designed to show that Johnson could also be tough with the Communists.

Second, Fulbright accepted Johnson's version of the alleged attacks on American ships in the Gulf of Tonkin. He would later learn that Johnson had lied about those events; it was clearly not the unprovoked aggression Johnson said it was. The fact that Johnson misrepresented the events, however, is not an excuse for Fulbright's grave mistake in having supported Johnson in the Tonkin crisis. Instead of trusting that Johnson was telling the truth, the legislative branch should have held hearings to uncover the facts. The administration was of course trying to rush the resolution through in a crisis atmosphere because hearings would have revealed that the administration's case was very weak.

The Tonkin resolution episode is indicative of Congress's willingness to let the executive branch dominate foreign policy. Although the resolution was frequently used to justify escalation of the war in the first couple of years, the administration eventually learned to use other excuses, such as the SEATO Treaty, the President's powers as commander in chief, and the passage of war appropriation bills for Vietnam. Senator George McGovern once told me in an interview that while the Tonkin crisis itself was not crucial, it was one important event among a series of important events in the Cold War in which the basic problem was Congress's deferential, often weak attitude toward the presidency on foreign policy issues. Fulbright was asked during the Tonkin debate whether the grant of power to the president was too sweeping. "What do we do if the President is not bent on peace, as you say he is?" he was asked. Fulbright replied, "Well, we can repeal it." True to his word, Fulbright did vote to repeal it in early 1966. He was overwhelmed in a vote of 92 to 5, however, which illustrates the political difficulties with which he was dealing.

His strategy throughout 1964 and 1965 was to support the President publicly while privately dissenting and advising him not to escalate the war. It is clear that Fulbright was dead wrong in this strategy. Only public dissent that would mobilize political opposition to the escalation could have influenced Johnson.

Belatedly, in early 1966, Fulbright began the time-consuming and arduous task of changing public opinion on the Cold War and on Vietnam. Although I criticize Fulbright for thinking that he could influence Johnson privately, it should be noted that he did offer some guarded public criticisms of the escalation even in 1965. He was bitterly critical of the anti-Communist intervention in the Dominican Republic in 1965, for example, yet it was still considered very controversial when Fulbright voted to repeal the Tonkin Gulf Resolution in early 1966.

Another illustration of the deep controversy sparked by his dissent occurred when Fulbright held hearings on American policy with respect to mainland China in March 1966. John King Fairbank and most other prestigious China scholars in the country appeared at those hearings. Although these scholars were critical of the Johnson administration's policies toward China and rejected the idea that China was a relentlessly expansionist power akin to Nazi Germany, they were reluctant to say anything critical of the U.S. Vietnam War policy. Fulbright pressed them to draw the logical conclusions of their criticism of the China policy, but they refused to go along. Fairbank admitted later in his memoirs that Fulbright had tried to press him to criticize the Vietnam policy because at the time, Dean Rusk was justifying the escalation in Vietnam as necessary to stop the expansion of Chinese communism.

The only exception to the rather ambiguous testimony at the 1966 China hearings was that of Hans Morgenthau, who did criticize both the Vietnam *and* the China policies of the United States. The China hearings are disturbing to university scholars because they tend to think of themselves as smarter than the general public and either smarter or freer to speak their minds than politicians are. In this case, however, Senators Fulbright and Wayne Morse were both quite blunt in opposing the Johnson administration's policies, whereas the professors seemed to be afraid of being labeled nonconformist. Fairbank also said that he did not want to be drawn into a debate between legislative and executive branches. Thus, Fulbright should be given some credit for his opposition to the war, belated though it was. He opposed the war for seven years, and through these hearings, speeches, and articles, he eventually played an important role in turning public opinion around.

The weak link in Fulbright's career was his civil rights record. This aspect of his career is the most controversial one. Randall Woods wrote in his book *Fulbright: A Biography* (1995): "That J. William Fulbright was a racist was indisputable." That statement is probably the most superficial one ever written about Senator Fulbright. If the word *racist* has any meaning, it should be applied to people such as Theodore Bilbo or Mark Furman. It is supposed to either mean that members of a given race are inferior or that hostility is being expressed toward them as a group. Another sentence in Woods' book admitted that Fulbright judged people of different races on their individual talents, which obviously contradicts the view that he was a racist.

Instead of simply condemning Fulbright as a racist, the more intelligent question would be, Could Fulbright have gone further than he did in opposing the segregationists in Arkansas? I believe that he could have. The episode for which he has received the most criticism was his silence regarding Governor Orval Faubus's demagoguery in the Little Rock Central High School crisis in 1957. That episode surpassed the debate on the liberal versus conservative approach to handling civil rights issues. It questioned whether one will stand up for the rule of law and oppose efforts to incite mob violence.

Fulbright tried to depict his choices at that time in fairly simplistic ways. He would say that he could either take a flaming liberal Hubert Humphrey stance on the civil rights issue or he could take a conservative stance. Actually, those positions were not his only alternatives. There was also what was described as the "southern moderate" approach, which his friend, Congressman Brooks Hays, adopted. Fulbright would respond to that suggestion by noting that Congressman Hays was defeated for reelection in 1958. Hays had defeated a segregationist opponent in the Democratic primary in that year and thought that he would easily be reelected because there was no appreciable Republican Party at the time. The Faubus machine engineered a write-in candidacy for a segregationist named Dale Alford, however, thereby gaining the element of surprise. It also used a series of electoral irregularities to gain voters. For instance, some of its people pretended to be election officials and distributed pre-printed stickers to voters with a check by Alford's name. In spite of these efforts, Hays lost that election by only 1,200 votes. One can only speculate what would have happened if Fulbright, who was then a very popular and powerful man, had stood with Hays. Fulbright would not have had to take a liberal position; he could have simply said, "I don't like the *Brown* decision any more than most of you do, but it is the law of the land, and we need to support it." That is what Congressman Hays was doing.

This issue is the greatest black mark on Fulbright's record, and it calls into question whether he would have been a great president. I think he would have been a good one, but he lacked sensitivity on the question of civil rights, which was the most important domestic issue of the day. Another reservation about whether he would have made a great president stems from his role as a dissenter and a gadfly. To be effective, a president must play the role of coalition builder and molder of public opinion. Fulbright probably served the Republic better in his role as an intellectual dissenter than he would have done as president. He is remembered throughout much of the world, especially in countries like India and Japan, for the Fulbright Program and for his record as the conscience of America. He is still seen as the man who implored Americans to think unthinkable thoughts and who warned against the arrogance of power. It is probably fortunate for him and for the country that his career turned out the way it did—that he was confined to the U.S. Senate.

QUESTION: Did Fulbright later look back on his civil rights record and ask himself whether he had handled the issue poorly? Or did he try to justify his actions under the circumstances?

MR. POWELL: Regarding his stance on the issues of the 1950s, he tended to justify it more than apologize for it. He often said that if he had taken a courageous stance on civil rights, he would have been defeated by one of the Faubus people, which would not have accomplished anything. He often pointed to Hays' defeat. Overall, his tendency was to continue rationalizing his position.

To be fair to Fulbright, I should add that later in his career he did begin to see the great importance of civil rights, and he did have some impressive accomplishments in that field. For example, he was one of only 6 Southern senators to vote for the confirmation of Thurgood Marshall to the Supreme Court. He also played a crucial role in blocking the nomination of G. Harold Carswell, who was probably the worst nominee in the history of the Supreme Court. That vote was very close, and had Fulbright not opposed Carswell, there might have been a full-fledged racist on the Supreme Court.

He favored Clement Haynsworth, but most of the law professors I talked to regard Haynsworth as a fairly respectable judge. In the words of Mike Klarman, "He got a raw deal." The accepted view is that he was not as bad as Carswell.

Also, Fulbright opposed Nixon's condemnation of the federal courts on the busing issue, which is impressive because there was nothing to gain politically by taking that stand. Actually, Fulbright had rather fatalistic views on the race issue. Even though he did not think busing was a good solution, he felt that Nixon was going too far in condemning federal courts, so he stood against it.

QUESTION: I read that toward the end of his life, Fulbright considered appointing convicted Whitewater financier James McDougal as his business adviser or manager. Can you tell us about his association with McDougal and Bill Clinton?

MR. POWELL: Fulbright actually lost a large amount of money in business relations with McDougal. Like everyone else, he was foolish enough to become involved with him as a business partner. I can relate one comical episode. My father, who was the editor of the liberal and now defunct *Arkansas Gazette*, once had a luncheon with McDougal and Fulbright. They tried to get my father to invest in a real estate scheme at Castle Grande. That illustration shows that McDougal and Fulbright were terrible businessmen. Although my father was a good editorial writer, he was not a businessman, yet he had the good sense to refuse their offer.

McDougal was fairly prominent in Little Rock. In the Arkansas campaigns, he played a somewhat important role. The most important people working for Fulbright, however, were Lee

Williams, Fulbright's administrative assistant in Washington; Seth Tillman, a "think tank" guy who is now professor at Georgetown; Carl Marcy, the chief of staff of the Foreign Relations Committee; Pat Holt, a Latin America specialist; and Clyde Pettit, who had been a journalist in Vietnam in 1965 and had predicted disaster if the United States escalated the war.

Fulbright appointed Clinton to his staff when Clinton was a student at Georgetown, and it was an excellent educational experience. Clinton wrote a fairly long paper on the Gulf of Tonkin episode while working for Fulbright, and he was present during the hearings. Clinton gained much exposure to foreign policy issues in that job, contrary to what some people think. He also went on many trade missions when he was governor. True, other presidents have had much more foreign policy experience than Clinton. Clinton first met Fulbright during the same Boys State delegation at which he met Kennedy. Fulbright was a role model for Clinton and was the person who gave him his start in politics. Clinton ran for Congress in 1974 against John Paul Hammerschmidt and has said that he would have supported Fulbright when he was defeated by Dale Bumpers if he had not been too tied up in his own race. Over the years, they continued to communicate. In early 1993, Fulbright advised Clinton not to order unilateral U.S. intervention in Bosnia, which I think was a wise decision. The situation has changed since then; now there is a cease-fire and a multilateral intervention force, so Fulbright would not have been as worried.

NARRATOR: How did Fulbright choose people such as Carl Marcy and Pat Holt for his staff? Were they in staff positions elsewhere in Congress?

MR. POWELL: He had a network of contacts, primarily through his university ties. He had been a George Washington law professor, and he often communicated with the east coast professors, who thought highly of him. Connections with the universities as well as the usual Arkansas connections were important in recruiting staff members. If an able man being considered also had good political connections, he was added to the staff.

NARRATOR: Did Fulbright experience a personal transformation during his life? I have read that he was rather conceited and arrogant as a young man. Since he came from an affluent family, he was supposedly very sure of himself. You said that this attitude changed over time. We saw an aspect of it when he came down a year before he died and spoke as part of our oral history project on Lyndon Johnson. He had mellowed, I thought. Among other things, he said that the accomplishment of which he was proudest was the Fulbright Program. He also admitted that on a few issues, he had been wrong.

MR. POWELL: He always regarded the Fulbright Program as his greatest accomplishment. I am not sure whether that assumption is correct or not. His dissent on the Cold War and the Vietnam War may have been his greatest accomplishment.

Regarding his so-called arrogance, I found that he was quite amiable most of the time and was easy to talk to about intellectual issues if he were in a relaxed mood. Talking about civil rights with him was difficult, naturally, because I disagreed with him strongly on that issue, and he hated to talk about it. In fact, I talked with him for many hours over the years and rarely discussed the subject of civil rights. Finally, I asked him to engage in some long discussions on that subject, and although he did not throw me out of his office, he was not eager to talk about it. I asked whether he might have assisted Hays in 1958, and he replied, "Well, you can speculate about that, but I have no desire for martyrdom." I think that statement encapsulates his view. When he was uncomfortable talking about an issue or in an unpleasant situation, such as when he was campaigning and people crowded around, he could make some rather arrogant remarks. When he was with people he knew or was interested in talking to, however, he could be very charming. I did not find him very arrogant in comparison to most of the politicians I have known, and I have known many of them.

NARRATOR: It was during his Rhodes scholar days at Oxford that people thought he was arrogant. Did he feel a need to demonstrate his intelligence to disprove the presumption that his mother and others had used social influence to promote his career?

MR. POWELL: People did think he was arrogant as a law professor. Federal judge Henry Woods was a brilliant student of
Fulbright and has written legal textbooks that are used around the
country. He told me that Fulbright was distant and seemed rather
concerned with showing off his brilliance. This behavior occurred
during the Depression when the social and economic gap between
Fulbright and the students was massive and he did not do anything
to bridge that gap. In contrast, some of the other law professors
would invite students to their houses. Also, he often used the
Socratic method to teach, which can be intimidating to students
unless it is balanced with some lecturing. If not careful, one can
become arrogant using that approach.

As president of the university, he became more popular with
the students. He probably became less arrogant because he did not
have the constant burden of teaching small numbers of students,
where he was conscious of making sure everyone knew how brilliant
he was. As university president, he was known as the former
Razorback football star, and he did not have to teach using the
Socratic method. When he was fired, there was a great outpouring
of sentiment in his favor. Throughout his career, various comments
were made on the issue of whether he was arrogant or amiable and
a courtly gentleman.

NARRATOR: Would he have had difficulty as president because he
had trouble suffering fools gladly?

MR. POWELL: Yes, I think so. He would not have had much
patience with a less intelligent congressman opposing one of his bills
for reasons that were not particularly rational. It is difficult to
imagine him enjoying coalition-building as FDR did. He enjoyed
dramatic gestures such as voting against Joe McCarthy, where he
was obviously so right and everyone else was so wrong, or writing
a brilliant speech condemning the "arrogance of power," as he did
in 1966 when most people were still going along with the Vietnam
War.

QUESTION: What was his political base in Arkansas that enabled
him to keep getting reelected despite these handicaps?

MR. POWELL: People in Arkansas loved the fact that he was a Razorback football star. He was a member of the aristocracy, so he could relate to the other wealthy and influential families around Arkansas. He could be a good speaker and rather charming when he wanted to be. He was able to get support from the small farmers because he was more supportive of them. At the same time, he could dilute some of the agribusiness opposition because he had personal contacts with the wealthier plantation owners and the big corporate farmers.

He was able to deflect part of the conservative opposition because he made so many compromises on the civil rights issue, they could not use that issue against him. For example, a key supporter of ex-Klansman Homer Adkins during the 1944 Senate race was legendary kingmaker Witt Stephens, a wealthy investment banker in Arkansas. Eventually, Fulbright made it clear that he would support the right wing on the civil rights issue, and Stephens joined him and remained loyal to him from then on. Protecting his right flank on the civil rights question was very important to Fulbright.

Toward the end of his career, that strategy became much less important. It is ironic that the man who finally defeated him in 1974, Dale Bumpers, was actually more liberal than he was on the race issue.

QUESTION: Did Bumpers do anything special to defeat him?

MR. POWELL: Fulbright was perceived as someone who spent all of his time on international affairs, especially the last five or six years of his career, and that perception was quite deadly to him in Arkansas. Also, he had taken many controversial positions over the last ten years of his career. His opposition to the war in Vietnam antagonized the right wing so thoroughly that they were ready to vote for anyone other than Fulbright. Bumpers simply ran a bland campaign, drawing support from all of the people who hated Fulbright and then splitting the progressive and middle-of-the-road vote with him.

QUESTION: Do you see any similarity between Senator Fulbright and President Johnson regarding their personality or methods of working?

MR. POWELL: No, I think they were different in their personalities. Johnson was a coalition builder who could be persuasive at times but could also use intimidation. When Fulbright tried to gain support from other senators, he would basically try to reason with them. If they agreed with him, fine, and if they did not, that was fine with him as well. If Fulbright had a strong interest in getting a bill through Congress, however, he could work with people and be fairly adroit. One such exception to his usual practice was the Fulbright Program. He knew that if he pitched it as a high-profile idealistic effort to send American youths abroad, the neanderthals in Congress would oppose him. It is interesting that the Honorable Kenneth McKellar of Tennessee later said that if he had paid attention to it at the time, he would have opposed the Fulbright Program as something that would subject American youths to dangerous ideas like communism, socialism, or other foreign "isms." Fulbright was clever in keeping it a low-profile item and financing it solely through the sale of surplus property abroad.

NARRATOR: How did you complete your work when you wrote the book? Do you generally work as a lone person? You must have interviewed many people to obtain all of your quotations.

MR. POWELL: I was quite busy writing it, and yes, I did many interviews. I think, however, that documents are more important and reliable than interviews for various reasons. People being interviewed may have memory problems or they may try to put a good spin on whatever they say. My father and I talked to Fulbright literally hundreds of times over a period of decades, so that was a good base of information with which to work. I would say the most important documents were the Fulbright papers, copies of the *Congressional Record*, and reports from congressional hearings.

Lee R. Powell

NARRATOR: We are very grateful to Mr. Powell for this most informative session on Senator J. William Fulbright.

III

STATESMEN AS THE CONSCIENCE OF SOCIETY

CHAPTER SEVEN

Morris Udall*

STEWART L. UDALL

NARRATOR: Stewart Udall was secretary of the interior from 1961 to 1969. He earned his law degree from the University of Arizona and practiced law in Tucson from 1948 to 1954. He then served in Congress from the Second District of Arizona from 1955 to 1961. He was counsel for the firm of Christopher and Phillips and became a syndicated columnist, writing "Udall and the Environment" beginning in 1970. He has served on the board of directors of Overview Corporation since 1969 and on several other boards. He was the author of *The Quiet Crisis* (1976), *Agenda for Tomorrow* (1968), *America's National Treasures* (1971), and *The National Parks of America* (1972). The book that he will be discussing during his presentation today is *The Myths of August: A Personal Exploration of Our Tragic Cold War Affair with the Atom* (1994). He will also discuss the life and works of his brother, Morris Udall.

MR. UDALL: I am fascinated with history. One story I have is about Senator Barry Goldwater, my brother, and myself. The three of us had a personal liking for one another, almost an affection, perhaps stemming from our common heritage as old pioneer

---

Presented in a Forum at the Miller Center of Public Affairs on 9 February 1996.

Arizona families. People could never understand how such ideological opposites could get along. In fact, in 1958 when Goldwater was reelected senator and we each got about the same vote percentage, people would ask how that could happen. Arizona people simply like independent-minded people.

When President Reagan nominated the first woman to be on the Supreme Court in 1981, Sandra Day O'Connor from Arizona, Barry Goldwater was as proud as if his own daughter had been nominated. The "piranha" press got busy, as one would expect, and discovered some "horrible" things about Judge O'Connor. While serving in the Arizona legislature, she had voted "wrong" on an abortion bill, and even more "heinous" was the fact that she had been the president of Planned Parenthood in Phoenix for nearly a decade, just as Senator Goldwater's wife had been before her. The Reverend Jerry Falwell was popular then, and he held a press conference announcing that he was sure President Reagan did not know about these things and that if every good Christian would write the President a letter or send him a wire, he would withdraw O'Connor's name.

Soon thereafter, Senator Goldwater was confronted by the press, and as one would expect, he did not budge an inch. In fact, he was outraged. Goldwater said Falwell did not know what he is talking about and deserved a "kick in the ass." My brother saw the quote in a Washington newspaper, scribbled a note, and had it hand-delivered to Barry. The note said, "Barry, it is a great idea, but it won't work. Falwell is a good Christian—he will turn the other cheek!"

My brother and I grew up in a small town located on the Colorado plateau about halfway between Petrified Forest and Zuni. This area is the only place where the Mormons and the Catholics came together. Brigham Young, in effect, met with Bishop Lamy, the Catholic archbishop that you read about in Willa Cather's *Death Comes for the Archbishop* (1922). We did not fit together very well, I'm afraid. I have always felt that we grew up in the 19th rather than the 20th century because we did not have tractors; we had horses. We did not have electricity; we had oil lamps. Our fuel was wood, which we had to gather. Being so close to the land was a great way to grow up. There is much talk nowadays about crime and the need to restore a sense of community. But when one grows up in a small town, that person knows what a community is; there is mutual respect and a respect for order.

Mormons have a lay clergy, and our father thus wore two hats—he was the leading church elder in the region and also the county judge. Coming from the smallest county in the state, he was eventually elected to the State Supreme Court. When people ask me how I got my start, I have always said, "I was Levi Udall's boy." He was in some ways the most respected man in the state, and the same was true of Mo.

I was elected to Congress in 1954 and served for six years under President Eisenhower. Ever since then I have been watching politics from either a front-row seat or from the bleachers in later years. It has been a fascinating time to study politics and American life, particularly having come from a small town. You get elected to Congress, and suddenly you are elevated to the big time. Some of my friends said, "Stewart, you were in President Kennedy's Cabinet; we expected *you* to run for president, not your brother." They did not understand my brother. He was younger than me and there was a great deal of sibling rivalry. If I could play good basketball, he could do it even better. We were trial lawyers together, and we had to draw straws to determine who made the closing argument when we practiced law. He was always determined to do better than I, and he usually did.

In 1976, Mo began talking about running for president, and his staff began pushing him. He sort of pioneered the notion that members of the House could run a serious presidential campaign. There was an old Speaker of the House named Champ Clark, who ran in 1912 but was defeated by Woodrow Wilson in a prolonged Democratic convention. My brother had a great deal of political courage, which I talk about in my book, *Myths of August*. The debate over the war in Vietnam not only tore the country apart, it tore Congress apart. My brother called me in the early fall of 1967. I was in President Johnson's Cabinet, and Johnson expected unswerving loyalty. All presidents do—too much, maybe. Mo said that he could not support the Vietnam War anymore. He told me that he was going home to Tucson and would give a speech withdrawing his support. We had talked about it, and we did not have any big disagreements. I told him not to telegraph his punch but instead just to go home and give his speech. If he had announced that he was going to do it, the President would have jumped on me and told me to stop him. He did what I asked.

He was a very good trial lawyer. He could take a weak case and make it into a strong case. He was brilliant in making an argument. When he went home and made that speech, he took all of the arguments that President Johnson, Dean Rusk, Robert McNamara, and others were making to justify the Vietnam War policy, went through them one by one, and demolished them.

Mo was also very venturesome. In 1969 he challenged the old Speaker of the House, John McCormack, even though he was much younger and had only been in Congress for three terms. He had a following among the younger members of Congress. These old men were no longer effective in his way of thinking and should get out of the way. He lost by a margin of about three to one. Then he ran for House majority leader when Carl Albert left that post to succeed the retiring Speaker John McCormack two years later, and he lost again.

Some of his aides and some congressmen convinced him that he ought to run for president in 1976. When he told me he was considering it, as his brother, I of course splashed some cold water on him. I did not quite see what kind of political launching pad he had since he had never been a committee chairman.

He *had* started to play the role of a leader, however, and had shown his colors. He and John Anderson, the congressman from Illinois, were the co-authors of the law concerning federal financing of presidential campaigns. This legislation was one of the major post-Watergate reform laws and shows the kind of reformer Mo was.

A small group of 10 or 12 people from New Hampshire who had been involved in earlier presidential campaigns decided that if they got together and picked the right candidate, they could choose the next President of the United States. Though they may not have thought of it quite that way, that is basically what they were thinking. The word got out, and they interviewed the candidates: Jimmy Carter, Senator Birch Bayh, Senator Fred Harris, Sargent Shriver, my brother, and some others. They liked Mo as a person, and they liked his approach to policy and everything else, so they decided to support him. Here he was, a relatively unknown congressman who did not have much power, but he came in second in New Hampshire, beating these prominent nationally known figures. Mo told me that these people in New Hampshire thought he could win, and I could not talk him out of running. I do not think President Carter ever forgave him for not dropping out of the race.

The campaign financing law came into being around this time, under which the federal government matches modest-size contributions. (Senator Dole and other candidates are currently waiting for the matching money to become available.) The Udall campaign had done something that no one else did in that 1976 campaign. Through direct mail, the staff developed a list of about 80,000 names from all over the country. When the campaign ran out of money to pay experts, I wrote letters every two weeks to get another $100,000 to be matched so we could continue down the campaign trail. My brother lost heart-breakingly close races in Wisconsin and Michigan, and those losses signaled the end of the story.

So many unanswerable questions remain, and Americans will never know if Mo would have made a good president. He had a special quality about him as an idealist, and he appealed to people. I would not compare him to Jack Kennedy, but with his sense of humor, he knew how to lose gracefully. In this country people judge the candidates' capacity to serve as president in the primaries each election year, which is what is happening right now. They hear what the candidates say and try to find out about their character and other kinds of information. Uncertainties always exist, and it is very difficult to make choices.

I was a liberal Democrat, a New Deal-type of Democrat in background and conviction. These types of Democrats had a way of looking down at President Eisenhower—he was not a Truman nor a Roosevelt. In retrospect, I think we were too hard on him. Some of my Democratic friends cannot understand me because I am an old man and I am trying to pry open my mind and take a fresh look. In writing my book on the Cold War, Eisenhower is the one who emerged as the outstanding figure who got us on a path with the Soviets away from nuclear war. He was the right president for the 1950s. The danger of some kind of nuclear war probably would have been greater if the United States had had the wrong kind of president. As I read him now, Eisenhower excelled in his steadiness, his capacity to keep the lid on military expenditures, and his beliefs about war and peace. After Stalin's death, he saw a window of opportunity. If Dulles had left him alone, he would have seized it. He recognized that nuclear war was suicidal and crazy. The great tragedy of his presidency was the U-2 affair in the final months, just as he was trying to initiate a regular series of summit meetings to reduce tensions in the Cold War. I see him in a different light now. The Cold War dominated my generation's lives for almost 50 years. It was the dominating issue in terms of budgets and always played a role in politics. In my book I wrote that Kennedy was too much of a Cold War warrior. Nixon certainly was. That election contest between them in 1960 is a fascinating study.

I thought the Cold War would drag on for years, and I worried, less so in the later years, that there would be some kind of violent outcome. It did not happen. Somehow, the U.S. government was wise enough to muddle through.

The most interesting, fascinating, and important book on the Cold War is one written by Ambassador Anatoly Dobrynin. He began his career as a young diplomat with Stalin and Molotov and then served as U.S. ambassador from 1962 to 1986. This man was without guile. He saw all of the presidents and worked with the secretaries of state. He wrote all about how the Politburo worked in his own country. His book is worth all of the big, thick books that former secretaries of state have written, including Kissinger's, in understanding what was actually occurring during the Cold War. With regard to the question of whether the U.S. officials were wise enough to make accommodations, Dobrynin rates Nixon very high, and I agree with his judgment concerning Nixon. This is not the "age of Nixon," as Senator Dole said at his funeral, however. Nixon is a puzzle people will never get past. According to Dobrynin, Jimmy Carter was a disaster in foreign policy. I could not find much with which to quarrel with regarding that analysis and judgment.

The end of a century is approaching, so I would like to look back at the last 100 years of American history. One way to judge presidents is by their vision and capacity to put forward ideas. The same criteria can be used to view people who wanted to be president or people who were leaders. One of the most important persons in the last half-century was Rachel Carson, whose ideas marked the beginning of what is now called the environmental movement. That movement has given Americans a new set of values and a different window to look at the world and contemplate the future. It did not just suddenly emerge on Earth Day. All great movements begin with an idea, and if the idea has validity, it catches on and grows. For example, the origin of what became the Progressive Movement—the idea that the country should have an income tax and the direct election of senators and that the government should become more involved in regulating the economy—began with the William Jennings Bryan campaign in 1896. I read what H. L. Mencken wrote about Bryan, and I remember Bryan and the Scopes trial. I never thought much of him.

Teddy Roosevelt and Woodrow Wilson promoted some parts of the progressive agenda, which came to life again in the New Deal. Those people who lived through the Great Depression and then World War II had tough experiences. I sometimes wish the American society was not so affluent; our children and their children could then learn from some of the experiences that the older generation had. Communities were stronger in the first half of the century, and the Depression made communities and families stronger.

I am a rather troubled supporter of President Clinton, as one would expect of an old-time Democrat like me. He mentioned children 37 times in the State of the Union address. One would think he was running for sheriff or the school board. In fact, nearly all politicians, not just Clinton, are taking advantage of the crime issue. The seedbed of crime is in communities. Crime has been and always will be a subject of local administration, with juries and communities meting out justice as they see it.

Having that kind of rural background is another point in my brother's favor in trying to guess what kind of president he would have been. As I reflect on the presidents I have known and those

I have watched, certain values and character traits seem to make them good or great. What a contradiction Nixon was! He will always fascinate people with his strengths and weaknesses. The Miller Center's effort to ascertain the roots of great statesmen is very important for the country because often people build up the presidency too much. This tendency resulted from the war and the Great Depression. In the 1960s, 20 or 25 senators, many of whom I knew extremely well, were what I called true *United States* senators. They spent much of their time working on national issues, not simply taking care of the home state needs the way so many of them do now. If they were faced with an issue of the Cold War or an environmental issue, they would think as a national senator. They were about evenly divided between the two political parties. One of the last of them, Mark Hatfield from Oregon, one of my Republican friends, has just announced his retirement. Two others were senator Mike Mansfield from Montana and Senator George Aiken from Vermont, who had breakfast together every morning. They liked and respected each other. After breakfast one morning in 1967, a reporter asked them what they had discussed. They said they had decided that the United States should declare victory in Vietnam and bring its troops home.

Under the U.S. system of government, leadership comes from different quarters, and I do think that Mo Udall, in his own way, had some influence as a leader. Maybe Americans will discover at some future point whether he was a statesman or not. I was not sure Eisenhower was a statesman until I began to work on my book and looked at him in an open-minded way.

NARRATOR: What motivated you to write your book on the threat of nuclear radiation?

MR. UDALL: The older I get the more aware I am of how politics affects people. After Senators Mark Hatfield and Al Simpson from Wyoming and a couple of Democrats announced they would leave the Senate, I wrote them a letter and said I was glad they were quitting. I told them I had tried to get my brother to quit, without success. No one can get Senator Strom Thurmond to quit. Some of these people cannot imagine life after being a congressman or a senator. I wrote, "I hope you not only quit, but that you're going to go home." I mentioned that Senator Goldwater and I went home, and that it *is* possible to have a rich, fulfilling life after Congress.

It has been nearly 20 years now since I left politics and went back to my old profession. Mo Udall and I were trial lawyers for personal injury cases. We had a law firm called Udall and Udall. The firm took on hopeless cases and won a few. I had Mormon relatives in southern Utah who began to suspect that an excess of cancer cases existed among the people who lived downwind from the bomb testing sites. As a result, I became involved as a lawyer in radiation cases and learned more about radiation, bombs, and cancer than I ever wanted to know. I also became interested in looking at my government and how it had lied to the American people. During the Cold War, secret entities were created in the government. I began looking at the presidents and their behavior in the Cold War. I conducted this study not pretending to be a historian, although I have been trained as a historian, but as a personal memoir. I drew on my experience and what I had seen. I saw what the Cold War and all of this secrecy had done to our democracy. For those who are open-minded and who wonder whether some of their old judgments are right or wrong, my book might stimulate your thinking.

QUESTION: Since you and your brother, for better or for worse, are portrayed as fathers of the modern environmental movement in the United States, what role do you see for the peaceful use of nuclear power?

MR. UDALL: Because I did not feel I had enough knowledge to ask questions, I was always a supporter of nuclear power when I was in the government. I watched it emerge. The old Atomic Energy Commission crowd, Glenn Seaborg and his people, wanted to build the largest nuclear plant in the world, and they convinced me there was a way to bleed off the steam and have the largest desalinization plant in the world. They chose a site a mile off of Huntington Beach in southern California and very shrewdly put me in front as a sort of "drum major." A bill was passed the last year I was in office, but Southern California Edison, one of the best-run power companies in the country, later pulled the plug on the project, and it was not built. The site chosen was on the San Andreas fault.

Nuclear power is dead in this country for now. Advocates used to pretend there were no safety problems and claimed that they could take the waste and make it disappear or something equivalent. True, the French and Japanese are moving ahead, and the United States should keep an eye on them. As an environmentalist, the one scenario I see for the resurgence of nuclear power is if the greenhouse effect turns out to be real and the burning of fossil fuels has to be reduced. With all of the expertise in engineering in this country, it is amazing that the United States did such a sloppy job with nuclear power. I am not an ideologue on nuclear power. Many people are simply afraid of it and do not want to hear about it anymore. Glenn Seaborg, the physicist who discovered plutonium, wanted nuclear power to be the ultimate source of energy and called for a plutonium-based economy because then he would be the savior of the world. A great deal of semi-religious conviction was associated with that movement. Americans will have to start over with nuclear power, *if* it has a future, that is.

NARRATOR: To what extent was your brother's political career brought to an end because of poor health?

MR. UDALL: His health was what derailed his career. Our family is genetically predisposed to Parkinson's disease. I have five brothers and sisters. One has already died of Parkinson's, and Mo is waiting to die. His condition was not diagnosed until later in his life, and his disease was never concealed. In 1983 when his Parkinson's was already causing problems, he decided he ought to run for president. It took his best friends leaning heavily on him to convince him that people would never elect a person with Parkinson's disease for president and that he could not conduct a campaign. He might have had a chance at getting the Democratic nomination in 1984. No one could have beaten President Reagan in the 1984 general election, however.

NARRATOR: Thank you, Mr. Udall, for sharing your personal experiences of government with us, particularly your insights involving your brother Mo Udall.

CHAPTER EIGHT

Senator Edmund S. Muskie[*]

BERNARD ASBELL

NARRATOR: Bernard Asbell, who has recently retired as a professor of nonfiction writing at Penn State University, is the author of 14 books of nonfiction, mostly political biographies and historical narratives.   Two of his books were best-sellers in the United States: *When F.D.R. Died* (1961) and *The Senate Nobody Knows* (1978). Other books written by Mr. Asbell include *The F.D.R. Memoirs* (1973) and *Mother & Daughter: The Letters of Eleanor and Anna Roosevelt* (1982).

In addition to Penn State University, Mr. Asbell has also taught at Yale, the University of Chicago, and the graduate schools of Fairfield and Antioch Universities and has been a writer-in-residence at Clark University. He is past president of the American Society of Journalists and Authors, the organization of independent nonfiction writers. This organization named him its 1996 Author of the Year for his latest book, *The Pill: A Biography of the Drug that Changed the World* (1995).

The Senate Nobody Knows tracks Ed Muskie for two-and-a-half years as he ushers the Clean Air Act through the Senate. It is a marvelous account of the way the Senate works. The book has been

---

[*]*Presented in a Forum at the Miller Center of Public Affairs on 8 November 1996.*

used as a text to help understand Congress in political science and government courses at Berkeley, Yale, and other places. It is also eminently readable and therefore has reached a larger number of people than most treatises on politics. We are delighted to have Mr. Asbell speak to us on Senator Edmund Muskie.

MR. ASBELL: The American people have just endured and somehow survived the 1996 national election campaign that most of them will either never forget or will manage to forget as soon as possible. No matter how candidates protested that "my opponent is not my enemy," they were publicly assailed as enemies, and the landscape of democracy was left a bloody battlefield. The stupefying carnage made many people wonder: Has it always been like this? Must it be like this? The portrait I want to draw today of Senator Edmund Muskie is meant to illustrate that it does not have to be that way.

Early in 1975 my editor at Doubleday, Sam Vaughan, called to ask if I might want to do a book about Edmund Muskie and the United States Senate. Doubleday had a contract with Muskie for his autobiography. But 1975—three years after Muskie's serious run for president and one year before he came close to running again— was a high-pressure time in his life. He found it impossible to fulfill that book commitment but said that if they wanted to get someone else to write about him, he would cooperate in every way. That was the assignment that Sam asked me to take.

I have to say that Muskie did cooperate in every way. He gave me generous amounts of one-on-one talking time. I sat in on any meeting I requested to attend, whether with staff or visitors, including many closed committee meetings. I found that the Senate of 1975 to 1978 was a far more open place than I had imagined it to be. Muskie in no way guided or tried to influence what went into the book.

In preparing for today, I decided to look at his life through one small peephole rather than offer some large summary portrait of Muskie. I found him best revealed by the way he led a small group of senators, the Environmental Pollution Subcommittee of the Public Works Committee, through the years of preliminary work on the 1975 Clear Air Act.

Muskie emerged in the Senate, and to a large degree in the nation, as "Mr. Environment." The environmental issue had been thrust upon him before many people cared about it. Events soon threatened to make the environment a war zone, however—an opportunity for Muskie to develop a rare style of public leadership, particularly in the arts of accommodation, compromise, and debate, which in Congress have lately fallen upon hard times.

I will set the stage by relating the strange mishap that led Muskie to fall, so to speak, into the environment. As he told me, Lyndon Johnson, the Senate majority leader, was welcoming the new senator from Maine to Washington in 1958. Johnson was explaining sympathetically how difficult the first years can be—how a single vote can sometimes involve a terrible complex of conflicting principles and obligations. Johnson leaned into Muskie and intimated, "Many times, Ed, you won't know how you're going to vote until the roll call gets to the M's." Johnson then turned to a plan that was on his mind to change the Senate rules for breaking a filibuster. The old rule, cherished by the South, required a two-thirds vote of all members—67 votes—for terminating the debate. Senate liberals were pressing to reduce that requirement to a three-fifths rule—60 votes. With neither side willing to give, Johnson had devised a compromise that would retain the requirement of a two-thirds vote, but two-thirds of only those members present. His impassioned explanation to Muskie was unmistakably an instruction as to how Johnson expected the newcomer to vote. Muskie absorbed the lecture silently. Finally Johnson said, "Well, Ed, you don't seem to have much to say." With a Maine reserve, Muskie replied, "The roll call hasn't got to the M's yet."

Johnson knew how to take care of a young upstart. He ignored Muskie's request for membership on the Foreign Relations Committee, and his second and third choices, Commerce and Judiciary. Muskie was banished to what seemed the Siberias of Public Works, Government Operations, and his fourth choice, Banking and Currency. In later years, Muskie's relations with Johnson improved but remained forever distant and guarded, and he attributed it to that moment.

The punishment was not over. Every committee member gets a subcommittee to chair, and Muskie's assignment was to head the

Public Works Special Subcommittee on Air and Water Pollution. Scarcely anything could have been less interesting at that time, but any subcommittee becomes what a resourceful senator can make of it. To discover his possibilities, Muskie scheduled hearings on air and water in 1963, 1964, and 1965. He held them in Detroit, Kansas City, New York, San Francisco, and Atlanta, not so much to collect a constituency as to see what he could learn and what people felt about his subject. The results were not always encouraging. In New Orleans, one woman urged the erection of a fence down both sides of the Mississippi River from Minnesota to the Gulf of Mexico to discourage bums from heaving beer cans into the river.

Muskie's subcommittee wrote the Clear Air Act of 1965, the first law concerned with poisons emitted by motor cars. It was a modest law, but by 1970 Muskie devised a novel way to strengthen it without risking the combined lobbying fury of industrial polluters. The bill won the support of President Richard Nixon, and it passed both houses of Congress with surprising acceptance. The magical invention of Muskie's committee was to avoid telling polluters exactly what they were to do to cleanse the air. Instead, the law stated *goals*, targets for dramatically reduced emissions by 1975, five years down the road. While mandating that motor cars and smoke-stacks must reduce pollution by 90 percent by the five-year expi-ration date, the law dictated not a word about the technologies or techniques for doing so. The truth was that neither Muskie nor the auto companies nor the National Academy of Sciences knew how to do it. Muskie's theory was that by threatening punishments if the specified targets were not achieved, the law could push, pull, and cajole polluters into inventing new technologies that would accom-plish the difficult job. The theory, which he called "forced technology," directed itself at a mortally serious goal. The National Academy of Sciences held air pollution in the 1960s responsible for 15,000 deaths and four million man-days of illness every year.

That clever 1970 Clean Air Act led to a confounding and unex-pected consequence, and no one knew just what to do about it. Muskie's unstated intention had been to force the auto companies to meet their targets by reinventing the internal combustion engine. Simultaneously, it was hoped, the new engine would consume less fuel, which would solve a related, but separate, problem of the time.

In the mid-1970s, fuel had suddenly vanished from world markets, causing long lines of cars at gasoline stations and something of a national panic.

The problem with those two politically popular goals—reducing both pollution and fuel consumption—was that they were mutually exclusive, or so said the auto companies. Worse still, the only known path to fuel economy was a smaller, lighter car, the kind that the Japanese were striving to put over on the American market. Through two years of clean air hearings, the preoccupation of the Big Three automakers, in an odd-couple partnership with the United Auto Workers union, was to fend off a smaller car, which would lead to significantly less profit and fewer jobs. But the industry stumbled over a way to observe the law without the heavy and chancy investment in a reconceived internal combustion engine. It adopted instead a new, albeit cranky, contraption called a catalytic converter. That converter, which you have on your can now, displeased the auto manufacturers almost as much as it did the man and woman in the street. It added to the car's price without increasing what Detroit reverently calls "customer appeal," thus further threatening the sales of American cars. Besides, the converter did nothing to conserve gasoline, but it did improve—minimally—the cleanliness of the air.

What were Muskie, his committee, and the Congress to do? Get tougher and turn the technological screws tighter? Automakers and smokestack emitters were on their knees demanding mercy, claiming that the technology for fully meeting the law's standards *did not exist.* The auto industry pleaded for more time, insisting it could not meet the proposed standards for 1978 models. Maybe they could do better if given a five-year delay. In 1975, Muskie and his committee had only a few months to decide, or the law would expire and there would be no Clean Air Act at all. Whose pleas against strangulation and death should be heeded, those of the victims of emphysema and heart disease, or the auto industry, which was indeed the economic lifeblood of millions? To make the choice even harder, there is no point at which one can say that the air is clean. It took Muskie's committee many months to realize that this decision was not scientific or technical. It is a *political* decision of how to clean the air and at what expense to make it politically acceptable.

In taking up the Clean Air Act renewal of 1975, Muskie's committee found itself assaulted by some of the most complicated alliances of lobbyists in all of history. An observer could scarcely tell the good guys from the bad guys. I sat in one secret meeting in which Henry Ford II and the UAW president, Leonard Woodcock, embarrassed in each other's presence but lobbying side by side against the Clean Air Act, urged Muskie to promise he would mention to no one that they were there together. Dancing arm in arm to the same rhythms as the National Association of Manufacturers and the U.S. Chamber of Commerce, they were opponents, not surprisingly, of the Sierra Club, Friends of the Earth, and Ralph Nader, newly inspired by Rachel Carson's book, *Silent Spring*, and the first Earth Day, which had ignited the youthful environmental movement. As one example of the strange bedfellows made by this campaign, almost no one knew that the altruistic Sierra Club was accepting cash subsidies for their lobbying contributed by a self-seeking multinational giant, the Englehard Minerals and Chemicals Corporation. That company mined and marketed platinum, the precious metal required by catalytic converters for cleaning the bad breath of automobiles. For them, the Clean Air Act and its catalytic converter was a profit bonanza. Even more confusing, the Mortgage Bankers Association, along with the International Council of Shopping Centers, were lofting the flag of environmentalism—and the catalytic converter because one proposed alternative to the catalytic converter was to clean the air by imposing heavy bridge polls in commercial areas and by limiting the size of parking lots. Either of these steps would attack retail sales and therefore real estate values. This strange war among large interests raged around Muskie's little subcommittee.

Imagine the division, the side-taking, the name-calling that would have erupted in the confrontional atmosphere of the Congress just concluded—or for that matter, in a one-sided Democratic Congress that would habitually turn deaf ears to the pleas of industry. Yet, Muskie's revised Clean Air Act was brought to a startling, relatively harmonious victory—not in 1975 as planned, but a year later in the closing moments of the session in 1976.

Especially after the election year Americans have just endured, this nation would profit by studying Muskie's virtuosity in the legislative process in seeking the precise point of potential harmony among contenders. Muskie loved nothing more, after committing himself to a difficult position on any issue, than to maneuver himself into the moderate position. Often I heard him make the following statement, one that is basic in understanding Muskie: "If I can control the positions of the extremes, I can control where the middle is and always win." I will add that when a more recent political celebrity, Dick Morris, applied the new name of "triangulation" to that very strategy and sold it to Bill Clinton as a campaign instrument, it worked.

Sitting opposite Muskie in his subcommittee, ideologically as well as physically, were James Buckley of New York, as devotedly right wing as his famous brother, columnist and editor William Buckley, and James McClure of Idaho, a bright and quiet lawyer whose main concern always was cost-benefit ratios, and someone did have to raise those measurements. On Muskie's side of the table sat a self-assured freshman, Gary Hart of Colorado, whose righteousness of purpose was matched only by the immaculacy of the air he espoused. If he was not always a Muskie ally, he was valuable in positioning the other extreme.

During the two-and-a-half years and scores of hours of close observation, I never heard a confrontive, destructive dispute erupt among these contenders. Rather than interpret how Muskie worked his art, I have created a monologue by stringing together a number of direct quotations from hours of observation and conversation with Muskie, thus letting him speak for himself in his own words, either in private conversation with me or things said to the committee:

"When I got a subcommittee of my own," he told me in his typical understatement, "it just seemed to me it would be better to invite the others to get involved; to accept their ideas as though they were truly members of the committee, which is not always the case around the Senate. So that has been the style of the subcommittee ever since it was created, and it has worked."

"But why," I asked, "would Buckley and McClure, as conservative on other issues as they are, be so open to cordiality with you on a contentious issue like clean air?"

Muskie's reply was:

> Senators who are disposed to conservative-liberal divisions could easily divide on the clean air issue along ideological lines, but if you don't put a label on things you can get people to look at the merits. As governor, I didn't label my programs as Democratic programs or as New Deal or liberal programs. Maine people aren't oriented that way. I talked about problems, practical options: What to do about this problem? Is this a sensible approach? So they adopted a lot of ideas which they might have rejected if the ideas had been labeled. People don't require labels. That's the point. Only politicians and political activists do. Once they sell something politically with success they try to pin a label on it so they can sell everything else under the same label, like selling a line of canned goods. But it is true, if those labels are used over and over again, after a while people start to measure programs in terms of the label. The trouble is the meaning of a label starts to change and then where are you? The Vietnam War, in the public eye, converted Hubert Humphrey from a liberal to a conservative. Nonsense! Liberal and conservative had nothing to do with that. Then the anti-war people were labeled the New Left without reference to other issues. I suppose my unhappiness with labels reflects my desire to get down to the substance of things. I'm receptive to any idea that will work.

This country has recently arrived at the opposite extreme, where someone can wave his hands and say, "liberal, liberal, liberal" and that would constitute a campaign, as has been seen in the last few weeks. The word *liberal* becomes the argument rather than the argument having substance.

Quoting Muskie again:

> I'm not averse, just because he's a conservative, to having Jim Buckley influence my judgment on pieces of legislation. He is going to have good ideas on this issue. On other issues, too, I'll listen. When he makes a point, it usually has intellectual

integrity. My previous view may be eliminated by what he has to say. If I don't accept his point of view I might alter my point of view to meet the objections he's raised. Why should I lose the benefit of that? If he has found the weak point and attacks it and his attack is credible intellectually, then I'm challenged to grapple with it and I think you just come out with sounder legislation.

A lot of people introduce legislation and they want it to come out exactly in the form they introduced it. When I introduce legislation it is simply to provoke a dialogue about the underlying complexities. To the extent that you can get the partisan or the liberal-conservative element out of this, you can have meaningful intellectual exchange, get people to focus on the issue. So I don't come before them with a *fait accompli*. I don't begin mark-ups ["mark-up" is a term that senators use for a working meeting of a committee, as against a hearing] saying "Now this is what I think we need to do." I let the thing evolve but I make proposals as we go along. I lay out issues, one at a time, to discuss and debate. So I will take initiatives but I don't try to put a full plate in front of them and say, "Now you eat all of this or reject it."

If Muskie ran into obstinacy in the two-year-long debate, it was not among committee members as much as among lobbyists, including those purporting to speak for the protection of the environment. Muskie could suffer rigidity from the auto industry lobby because he expected it, but the intolerance of differing viewpoints by the young environmentalists was harder to take, particularly when they cast Muskie as the enemy if he did not always run with their insistence on purity.

One night when a committee meeting arrived at a standoff and all agreed to take some time to develop new approaches, Muskie, suddenly directed his eyes away from his fellow members, glanced toward their audience of 50-or-so lobbyists and let loose a sermon he had apparently been storing up:

I would hope that something new develops among those who watch and listen. I hope that they're getting a chance to observe that no interest has all its own way in the development of legislation like this. There are conflicting interests, yet someone

141

representing a particular interest sometimes is disposed to think he can have his own way all through the legislation; that there is no need to give anything, just insist upon taking. I wish those who have an interest in legislation would address themselves just occasionally to trying to figure out what they can give in order to help achieve a balance. I've found [now he leaned forward, staring directly into the audience, not just commenting, but scolding now] more intransigence outside this committee than I've found within it. That does nothing but slow down the legislative process. I address that to anybody who would like to take it to heart.

The entire audience erupted in nervous laughter: Surely he meant someone else.

When they adjourned the meeting, they hoped something new would develop overnight. Something new did emerge the next morning: a successful compromise from an unexpected source, Senator Robert Stafford, a Republican of Vermont, who rarely attended committee meetings, and when he did, almost never uttered a word.

That night one of Muskie's staff people gave a candle-lit dinner party. The senator, his family away in Maine for the summer, attended. With unconcealed pride, he said, "You've got to watch out for those quiet canny northern New Englanders. It's often that the man who knows the least has a detachment to find where the area of agreement is." Someone else commented that he did not think of awkward, shy Robert Stafford as exercising power. "*Power, Power*," scoffed Muskie almost in a roar. "People have all sorts of conspiratorial theories on what constitutes power in the Senate. It has little to do with the size of the state you come from. Or the source of your money. Or committee chairmanships, although that certainly gives you a kind of power. The real power up there comes from doing your work and knowing what you're talking about. Power is the ability to change someone's mind. *That* is power around here!" Then, slamming a flat palm on the table, he concluded, "The most important thing in the Senate is credibility. *Credibility. That* is power!"

The word *credibility* was central to everything that Muskie thought and did. By his way of thinking, if the Clean Air Act was so "strong" that it invited either widespread noncompliance or repeated revisions of its standards and deadlines, the act would be disrespected and therefore would be *weak* and would actually contribute to a prolongation of foul air.

I asked Muskie what constitutes credibility in the Senate. His reply was ready:

> When someone gets up to say that something is so, and if you can have absolute reliance that he is right, *that* is credibility. And that is power. If you've done your homework and know what you're talking about, that is power. It takes time to build up. Over the years, that is one thing that has not changed in the Senate.

Many senators, he said, cannot see beyond confrontation politics. Their imaginations cannot handle anything beyond pitting strength against strength, one position merely outvoting another, defeating its valid points along with its less valid ones. Those statements characterize a great deal of what happens in committees. It may take less time, but in Muskie's view, there is nothing efficient about it.

Did the 1975 act, a two-year marathon and subcommittee, take too long? I asked him. Muskie's surprising reply: *It took that much time to bring out the disagreement.* The seeming disorder of long disagreement in Congress is, he argued, an *efficient* process. It is when agreement comes too soon, too easily, that Congress becomes inefficient. Disagreement, asserted Muskie, lifting his vocal sonority—he was elaborating his central theme—the clear *defining* of disagreement and the eventual *reconciliation* of disagreement is the main element of good legislation and therefore is efficient, no matter how long it takes. When a law goes through this process, particularly the reconciliation part, it comes out as a piece of strong and good legislation.

Let me add one last thought: The record for length of debate on the floor of the United States Senate is 88 days. Generally, a bill is not debated for more than two or three days, most for only three or four hours, because the work has taken place in committee. The bill that holds the record went to the floor and was argued, pulled apart, amended, and counteramended for 88 days until it was considered worthless, amended out of existence. That bill was the Civil Rights Act. It has never been amended since.

NARRATOR: Everett Dirksen would often say at the end of a debate, "Reasonable men can live with this."

QUESTION: I do not think markups were open to the public during the 1970 Clean Air debate, but they were open in the late 1970s. Did that change affect the style or outcome of the debates?

MR. ASBELL: The debates obviously were different. In comparison with courtroom situations today, when people hear that there will be a television camera in a courtroom, behavior changes. Some environmental lobbyists, people whom we would expect to welcome openness the most, told me that permitting them to attend the markups made the situation more difficult for them, although there were advantages as well. It was more difficult to make deals and come to quiet agreements. I never heard anyone say that it made a great difference on balance. It did change behavior, but I doubt that it changed the legislation very much.

QUESTION: Is the process you described of defining areas of disagreement in a group of relative equals also applicable in cases where the group consists of a leader and his followers? Examples of this process would include the president and his Cabinet or the president and vice presidents of a company.

MR. ASBELL: In an old Lincoln story, Lincoln always had his Cabinet discuss a decision he had to make and then take a vote. If they voted against what he wished, he would announce that he was overriding them with a "majority" of one.

In the combative Congress this country just had, no one bothered to listen to anyone else. Everyone was out to humiliate and crush the other side. I think that having the disagreement emerge in all of its meaning and all of its parts so that one knows with whom he or she is dealing is a superior life principle. Yet it took a great man to define it in just that way. To have the disagreement come out does tend to reduce the heat and may even tend to reduce the disagreement. Every married person who has ever had a spat at home knows that when a couple reaches an understanding based on what each of them is saying, either the disagreement largely disappears or at least they know more clearly what they have to straighten out.

QUESTION: What kind of president would Muskie have made?

MR. ASBELL: During those two-and-a-half years when I spent a great deal of time around Muskie and his staff, I thought about that question. At times I thought he should not be president because he had a temper. Then I learned that he become angry in the most deliberate, studied ways. He became angry when it would accomplish a purpose. Coming down heavily on members of his staff was his way of challenging them and testing their ideas.

I have developed a personal notion of one critical test of whether a public man has what it takes to be president. Can he run a successful campaign? A campaign is an enormously complex administrative and political act. Americans have just seen an example of a terribly run campaign by an otherwise outstanding politician. Bob Dole was a great legislator, but after watching his campaign, I think he would have made a terrible president. He cannot plan. He cannot use people or take advice. Muskie would have made a much better president than many we have seen.

QUESTION: Are there other reasons that he did not become president?

MR. ASBELL: First was the incident on the back of a truck in front of the Manchester, New Hampshire, newspaper building where everyone knows that Muskie cried. That was the end of Ed Muskie. Well, he did not cry. He was shaken and containing himself, but for whatever it is worth, he did not cry, and it would not have been disqualifying if he had.

Few people remember that Ed Muskie won the New Hampshire primary. The newspapers just decided in advance that since Maine is a neighboring state, Muskie had to get 65 percent of the vote or he would have done badly in New Hampshire. He got about 58 percent of the vote, and since he did not meet the journalistic expectations, he was in political disgrace. Losing favor that way is also a national judgment. We all have to take responsibility for it.

I think Muskie lost the nomination and probably would have lost the general election because it was a bad year for a moderate politician like Muskie. It was a year that chose McGovern to run against Nixon. It was an immoderate year and a bitter election, engineered largely by people on the left side of the Democratic Party and on the right side of the Republican Party. I think the Vietnam War had a great deal to do with that situation. It was a time of hard and intense feelings and one of wanting to throw things at the opposition. Such times are not good for people like Muskie, or for that matter, Bob Dole. This year Dole sensed that fact, but too late. He did not abandon moderation until the closing days of the campaign.

QUESTION: With respect to the present Congress, have you anything cheerful to report about how some of the senators and congressmen and congresswomen are working in the tradition of Muskie?

MR. ASBELL: I think the last two years have been the worst congressional exhibition in our lifetime. The extremes were so pulled apart that everyone was put on their worst behavior. There was no way in that atmosphere to "bring out the disagreement" so it could be defined and reconciled. The Gingrich Congress lived by a sports mentality: to defeat the other side. Their slogan, stated the first day, was "We'll cooperate, but won't compromise," whatever in the world that means.

COMMENT: They did manage to pass some legislation at the end.

MR. ASBELL: Yes, they did because they found out painfully that the other behavior did not work. The Republicans now accuse Clinton of having become a Republican by adopting what they proposed, but they also adopted much of what Clinton proposed. In other words, they all accommodated.

QUESTION: Was there any one person or any people who behaved more like Muskie to make this accommodation happen?

MR. ASBELL: If someone did so in the House, that person was invisible. I think on the whole that the Senate leadership behaved quite well. Dole behaved in his usual way as a legislator, and Trent Lott may turn out to be a good majority leader. I think Minority Leader Tom Daschle is an able man, and these people will now put the Muskie style of accommodation out front—trying to get done what it is possible to get done, not by trashing the other side, but by looking at any given situation and asking how much can be accomplished. That is how Muskie worked.

I will add a footnote that I think the Clintons learned a good lesson. The composition of that medical plan was monstrous—monstrous in terms of the ability of the American people and Congress to swallow that much. It just defies all of U.S. history, which is that changes are made incrementally. There are almost never wholesale changes, but progress by little bits—except for the 100 days of 1932 and the giant step of Social Security.

It is interesting that after three years in office, when Clinton took the small increment of his health plan that said if a person lost his or her job, he or she could take their health insurance with them, no one dared oppose it. It sailed right through Congress.

NARRATOR: We certainly want to thank Mr. Asbell for enlivening this place and inspiring us to think about some of the fundamentals of politics.

CHAPTER NINE

The Life of Nelson A. Rockefeller*

CARY REICH

NARRATOR: New York City resident Cary Reich is the author of a magisterial work, *The Life of Nelson A. Rockefeller: Worlds to Conquer, 1908–1958* (1996), which is the first volume in what will be a two-volume biography. The second volume is expected to be published in 1997. The biography is based on Cary Reich's original research into the Rockefeller family archives, FBI and FOIA (National Security Archives–Freedom of Information Act) files, and interviews with 300 individuals, many of whom previously had never spoken on the record about Governor Rockefeller. Reviewers are already comparing the book with the works of David McCullough, Doris Kearns Goodwin, and Robert Caro. The book was a finalist for the 1996 National Book Award in nonfiction.

Earlier in his career, Mr. Reich was the executive editor of *Institutional Investor.* He also authored numerous other portraits of the powerful and wealthy, including *Financier: The Biography of André Meyer* (1983). He has received a number of highly prized journalism awards, including the Overseas Press Award, the Deadline Club Award, and the John Hancock Award for Excellence in Business and Financial Journalism.

Presented in a Forum at the Miller Center of Public Affairs on 7 February 1996.

MR. REICH: Because of its enormous historical resonance, the name of Nelson Rockefeller is still frequently invoked in politics. To conservatives, he is still the greatest liberal bogeyman, the symbol of all that they detest. In the 1992 presidential campaign, for example, Colin Powell's candidacy incurred an enormous backlash from the conservative wing of the Republican Party once Powell was identified as a secret Rockefeller Republican. One conservative activist warned that if Powell got the Republican nomination, "it would be as if Ronald Reagan had never lived and Nelson Rockefeller never died." Another conservative reminded his audience that Powell's supposed role model was a conspicuous philanderer. Finally, in the course of the primaries, Pat Buchanan warned that there would be a floor fight at the convention if Bob Dole selected a Rockefeller Republican as his vice-presidential nominee.

At the same time, Rockefeller's name has recently been invoked in an approving way by other factions in the Republican Party, specifically Governors Christine Todd Whitman of New Jersey and William Weld of Massachusetts. Whitman has gone so far as to identify herself publicly as a Rockefeller Republican, which she describes as a Republican with a social conscience.

Whatever one's views of Nelson Rockefeller, there was an unavoidable sense that this man was a force, an outsized presence, a phenomenon rare in American politics. He set the standard—for better or worse—of the imperial, activist governorship. He was the singular embodiment of liberal Republicanism. He defined and dominated that wing of the party so much that his own downfall brought about the liberal wing's downfall as well. In fact, the liberal wing never recovered. Rockefeller also posed one of the great conundrums of 20th-century American history: How was it possible that someone with such vast gifts, such unbounded energy, such unlimited resources, and such deep, wide-ranging experience did not become president?

Rockefeller truly was an incredible figure, a fact that was as apparent in the years *before* he became governor as in the years of his greatest renown. For example, in the spring of 1953, Nelson Rockefeller joined the Eisenhower administration as undersecretary of the new Department of Health, Education, and Welfare, which

150

required him to resign from his positions and board memberships in the private sector. The sheer number of jobs and positions from which Rockefeller had to resign indicates the scope of his activities. They are, in alphabetical order: chairman of American International Association; vice president and director of Amun-Israeli Housing Corporation; member of the board of trustees of the Committee for Economic Development; chairman of the Council for Inter-American Cooperation; president of Hills Realty Company; president of International Basic Economy Corporation (IBEC); chairman of the IBEC Research Institute; chairman of IBEC Technical Services Corporation; director of Madigan Hyland, Inc.; president of the Museum of Modern Art; member of the board of the National Council for U.S. Art in the United Nations; vice chairman of the National 4-H Club Builders Council; vice president of the Pan-American Society of the United States; chairman of the executive committee of Rockefeller Brothers, Inc.; chairman of Rockefeller Center, Inc.; president of the Venezuelan Basic Economy Corporation; vice president of the Westchester County Board of Health. He did hold onto a few positions. He continued on the board of the Fresh Air Fund, as a trustee of the Union Church of Pocantico Hills, and on the board of the Seal Harbor Village Improvement Society.

This list provides a good snapshot of the world of Nelson Rockefeller circa 1953–five years before he became governor of New York, before he became the Rocky of legend and lore. The list also gives a glimpse of Rockefeller's inexhaustible energy. Although this period might be deemed a slow time in his life, he was running the Rockefeller Center, the Museum of Modern Art, a vast Latin American business empire, the Rockefeller brothers' joint philanthropic efforts, and the family estate in Pocantico Hills, as well as serving on a dozen public and private boards—including the board of the Seal Harbor Village Improvement Society. It is no wonder that I have already spent eight years and counting in tracking his life. On my desk I have an old Rockefeller gubernatorial campaign button that reads: "Rocky: He's Done a Lot. He'll Do More." It is as if Nelson Rockefeller is staring right at me saying, "You've Done a Lot. And You're Going to Have to Do a Lot More."

Nelson Rockefeller was a man whose engine was perpetually in overdrive well before he became governor of the Empire State. In the 1940s when he was FDR's coordinator of inter-American affairs, Rockefeller drove himself to work each morning, picking up a number of his subordinates along the way. Here is how one recalled the morning commute with Rockefeller: "He drove as if he were piloting a Parisian taxicab. He drove too fast. He drove too close to other cars. The rest of us were always mentally cringing and putting on the brakes. He didn't seem to give a damn." That was Nelson Rockefeller. A wife of one of his closest aides recalled, "I cannot picture him static, standing quietly. He was always in motion."

All who lived in the Empire State during the Rockefeller era saw that restlessness and relentless drive at work during his governorship. The public saw it in the vast array of programs that he launched. These programs addressed everything from health care to the environment, education, housing, the arts, and the state's transportation needs. It was seen in all of the agencies that he created during his governorship: the Housing Finance Agency, the State University Construction Fund, the Metropolitan Transportation Authority, the Adirondack Park Agency, the State Council for the Arts, and the Urban Development Corporation. It was seen as well in his monumental building programs around the state. Even today—and maybe especially today, in light of current Americans' attitudes toward government—the statistics are mind-boggling: 90,000 new low- and moderate-income housing units; 200 water treatment plants built to curb pollution; 23 new state mental health facilities. He also built thousands of miles of new highways—four-and-a-half miles for each day of the 15 years that he was in office. His crowning achievement was the great expansion of the New York state university system. When he assumed the governorship, there were 28 campuses educating 38,000 students; by the end of his governorship, 71 campuses were educating 246,000 students.

As I began to delve into this man's life, it was eye-opening for me to discover that this same juggernaut quality characterized the years before Rockefeller became governor, before he became Rocky. One person who accompanied him on a business trip to Venezuela said: "He goes a little like a mad man from daybreak until dusk and then he wants to talk things over with the experts until midnight." Another person who worked for him in the Rockefeller family office recalled: "He never stopped. He'd have all his memos read by eight in the morning, and then come into the office. By four-thirty you didn't mess with him. He was tired and ready to go home, but he was only ready to go home and freshen up for the set of players that were coming for the evening, all of whom tied into something else he was doing. He loved having multiple interests—huge multiple interests."

Many people found this high-octane display maddening. I loved Adlai Stevenson's comment about Rockefeller in the 1940s: "The trouble with Nelson is that he has so many ideas and they're so wonderful, but when you call him the next day about one of them he's on to something else or off to Venezuela."

The fact was that while many of his ideas would vanish into the ozone, an amazing number of them became real. His life is illustrative of one of George Bernard Shaw's epigrams: "The reasonable man adapts himself to the world; the unreasonable one persists in trying to adapt the world to himself. Therefore all progress depends on the unreasonable man."

It is truly incredible what this one very unreasonable man, Nelson Rockefeller, accomplished in the 50 years before he became governor. By the time he was 31, he had forced out the original management that had run Rockefeller Center and had put himself in charge. By then, he had also put himself in charge of the Museum of Modern Art, which was just coming into its own at that time. By the time he was 40, he had created a whole new government position for himself, the coordinator of inter-American affairs, and was overseeing the United States' wartime relations with Latin America. A few years later at the organizing conference for the United Nations, he helped create the framework for NATO and other postwar alliances. A couple of years after those accomplishments, he was the driving force behind Harry Truman's Point Four foreign aid program to the developing world.

Rockefeller was also very active in the administration of Dwight Eisenhower. He oversaw the first reorganization of the federal government since the New Deal, which included among other things the creation of the Department of Health, Education, and Welfare (HEW) and the United States Information Agency (USIA). As HEW undersecretary Rockefeller pushed through the most sweeping expansion of the Social Security system since its inception. Later, when he became special assistant to the President for Cold War strategy, he engineered the Open Skies program, which was probably the biggest Cold War propaganda coup of the Eisenhower era. All of these accomplishments and many more were made before he became governor of New York.

One famous F. Scott Fitzgerald quote in effect says, "There are no second acts in American lives." In Nelson Rockefeller's life, however, that was certainly not the case. There was a first act, a second act, and a third act. My book only covers the first act—Rockefeller's years before he became governor, which are as riveting as the later drama of his governorship and presidential bids.

I never intended for my Rockefeller biography to be a two-volume work, but as I researched and wrote, it became clear to me and to my editor at Doubleday that so much had happened in this man's early life that one volume could not possibly contain it all.

Much of what marked the man who became a national figure and New York's governor—the grandiosity, the energy, the insatiable hunger for ideas, the ruthlessness, the obliviousness to cost and consequence—was already on display in the young Nelson Rockefeller. He was political long before he went into politics.

His political savvy can be traced to his relations with his father, John D. Rockefeller Jr., who has been lost to history to some extent as a result of being sandwiched between his father, the great oil tycoon, and his overachieving sons, Nelson in particular. John D. Rockefeller Jr. was a formidable character in his own right, however. This was the man who built Rockefeller Center, the Cloisters, and Riverside Church. He was the man who preserved the Palisades in New York, Acadia National Park in Maine, and Grand Teton National Park in Wyoming. He was also the man who founded and shepherded most of his family's great philanthropic edifices.

Hanging in the dining room of the family seat at the Kykuit manor in Pocantico Hills is a portrait of John D. Rockefeller Jr., from which he glowers at visitors from behind his wire-rim spectacles. It is a painting that truly does him justice. A stern, forbidding character, he was probably sternest with his own children.

One good illustration of this sternness is a letter he wrote in the early 1930s to his older sons, John III and Nelson. By then, both sons were working for him in the family office, and at one point John pleaded with his father to make himself more accessible to them. In response, John Jr. wrote the following letter:

> Either before I went abroad or after my return when I had a luncheon talk with you boys I think I said . . . that you boys would always have the first call on my time for conference about any matter that you were seriously desirous of discussing with me. To that end I suggested that you . . . feel free to let me know any time when you had such subjects that you wanted to discuss and that I would at my early convenience appoint a leisurely time for such a talk. I cannot promise to arrange for such a conference at short notice . . . but I will always set a time at your request and that too at my early convenience.

That was John Jr.

Nelson's first great political challenge was to carve a place for himself in his father's well-regulated domain. What Nelson wanted most of all was to run Rockefeller Center, which was at that time still being built, but to do so would require displacing the management team his father had personally appointed. Rather than mount a direct challenge, which would have never worked with his father, Nelson launched a spectacular flanking maneuver. He created his own little business in a leased-out space in Rockefeller Center, and from that little niche he began to worm his way into his father's operations. He used that favorite bureaucratic device, the organizational study, to build up his position. He lined up a key strategic ally in his father's trusted counsel, Thomas Debevoise. Then, when he had all of his pieces lined up, he executed the coup d'etat, firing the managers and putting himself at the helm. It was so brilliantly and stealthily accomplished that his father, for all of his misgivings, was utterly helpless to do anything about it.

One tactic Nelson often used with his father was to praise him excessively. There are countless examples of Nelson buttering up his father, praising him, and declaring in the most obsequious ways how great a man he was and how unworthy he, Nelson, was by comparison. Some of this gushing prose is, frankly, nauseating to read, but that approach worked. What Nelson learned at an early age was that no matter how skeptical, no matter how worldly-wise, and no matter how hard-nosed his superiors were, they would almost always succumb to outrageous flattery.

Again and again he used this technique, first with his father and then with presidents and secretaries of state. When FDR was reelected in 1940, Nelson wrote a letter to Roosevelt—despite the fact that the Rockefeller family had backed Roosevelt's opponent, Wendell Willkie—saying, "Your reelection yesterday constitutes the greatest vote of confidence ever given any American." On another occasion, when Roosevelt was coordinator of inter-American affairs, he called Roosevelt to ask him if he had any objections to calling a recently established, federally funded scholarship program for Latin American students the Roosevelt Scholarships. FDR had no objections.

In another example, Nelson used this tactic of lavish flattery on FDR's secretary of state, Cordell Hull. Hull had just returned from a wartime conference in Moscow, and Rockefeller had rushed to the airport to greet him. Rockefeller followed up the meeting with the following letter to Secretary Hull:

> I can't tell you what a thrill I got when the wing of your great army plane swung out over the President's car and came to rest in front of the hangar, the door opened, and you stepped out, returning from the most significant trip that any American has made since the start of the war. . . . You have brought new hope and confidence into the hearts of the people in every home in this country.

Undoubtedly, the most egregious instances of Rockefeller's fawning were in his dealings with Dwight Eisenhower. At one point, Rockefeller, who by then was working in the administration, told Eisenhower that his new hobby was collecting Eisenhower's statements and speeches with a view toward publishing them. Rockefeller told the President by way of explanation that "it seemed to me that you expressed basic American beliefs on current issues with greater clarity and penetration than anyone since Lincoln."

Rockefeller did more than just flatter Eisenhower with sweet words. He also built a one-hole golf course at his home in Washington in the hope that he could lure the President there. Eisenhower never came. Nelson Rockefeller also paid out of his own pocket for the distribution of 20,000 official photographs of Ike to U.S. government offices around the world "as a public service." Most incredibly, while working for Eisenhower at the White House, Nelson continually plied the President with expensive gifts, all of which the President quite shamelessly accepted.

For example, Rockefeller bought the 18th-century table and chairs that Eisenhower had used at Stanwell House near London during the planning of the D-Day invasion and presented the furniture to the President in commemoration of the 10th anniversary of V-E Day. He also paid for the landscaping of Eisenhower's farm in Gettysburg. Eisenhower had casually mentioned one day over breakfast that his farm in Gettysburg was in need of some landscaping, and not long afterward Rockefeller brought in his own landscape architect to work on the grounds. Soon an impressive supply of trees began arriving at Gettysburg—oaks, elms, pines, spruces, red maples, and sugar maples—courtesy of Nelson Rockefeller.

Many people are probably astonished that a Rockefeller would resort to such shameless flattery, but I think the flattery is simply a measure of Rockefeller's ambition and his readiness to go to any length to achieve his ends. Among Rockefeller's papers at the Rockefeller Archive Center is a confessional letter he wrote to his mother when he was 24 years old. In the letter he speaks quite frankly of what he describes as his "overpowering ambition." He describes himself in that letter as hard and unfeeling. He also wrote, "If one is going to get very far in this world one must be impersonal and not waste one's emotional strength on irrelevant things. The result has been that I take a pretty cold attitude about most things." It is one of the rare times that Rockefeller indulged in a brutal self-analysis, let down that great gregarious facade, and showed the cold calculation that lay beneath.

The target of his ambitions was obviously the presidency. As he once admitted, he had been aiming in that direction "[e]ver since I was a kid. After all, when you think of what I had, what else was there to aspire to?" In my book I show that as early as 1953, before Rockefeller had been elected to any office and in fact before Dwight Eisenhower had been sworn in as president, Rockefeller had been positioning himself for a presidential run.

Unlike men such as Lyndon Johnson, however, Rockefeller was not after power for its own sake. He truly did see high office as a means to an end, a mechanism by which he could accomplish great things. He liked to view himself not as a politician, but as a problem-solver. "My interest is not really the politics," he once said when he was governor. "My interest is in the government and the administration, the solving of problems. I have a lot of energy. I have a lot of interests and I see a problem and I immediately start to think about a solution. Then I have to get someone who can work on that."

In many ways Nelson Rockefeller was a policy wonk long before that term gained currency. Both before and during his governorship, he loved brainstorming over policy and problems. Throughout his life he appointed and participated in task forces, study panels, and blue-ribbon commissions, not because they were politically expedient, but because he was energized by the give and take.

He truly believed that no problem was insoluble if enough brainpower—and enough money—were applied. As Henry Kissinger once told me when he was reflecting on Rockefeller, "Cynics don't build cathedrals." Nelson Rockefeller may have been many things, but he was never a cynic.

For Nelson Rockefeller, very little was impossible. When he needed the mantels over his apartment fireplaces decorated in the 1930s, he brought in Matisse and Léger. When he coveted a yellow Phantom Five Rolls Royce and was told by the company that only one had been made and it was not for sale, he had a British intelligence operative sneak into the Rolls Royce garage and scratch a paint chip from the car so that he could repaint a gray Rolls the exact same color. When a developer proposed to buy the financially troubled Knickerbocker Club and build a high rise on the site, thus threatening the view from Rockefeller's Fifth Avenue apartment, Rockefeller simply bought the Knickerbocker Club himself to prevent his view from being blocked.

His approach to government was just a natural extension of this mind-set. The lesson that emerged from the Rockefeller era in New York was that some problems were susceptible to this brains-and-money blitzkrieg—housing and higher education, for example. Others, however, were not as susceptible, the most obvious being the drug problem. Rockefeller's arbitrary, draconian drug laws—probably the toughest, most inflexible ever enacted by any state—were a product of his desperation after all of his standard approaches, such as study groups and the like, failed.

Another lesson that emerged from the Rockefeller era was that there is a big price to pay for the Rockefeller approach—namely, a huge state debt. The heedlessness that Rockefeller showed in his personal expenditures was similarly illustrated in his attitude toward the public purse. As his longtime attorney general, Louis Lefkowitz, told me, "If he wanted to spend money, money was no object."

Nelson Rockefeller really did believe that government had the answers—maybe not all of the answers, but most of them. When Christine Todd Whitman and others talk about Rockefeller Republicanism, they speak about its social consciousness and its quality of caring. Certainly, that quality was a good part of what Rockefeller represented, but what these nouveau Rockefeller Republicans ignore is that he was a tax-and-spend liberal for much of his career.

Also largely forgotten is Nelson Rockefeller's foreign policy side. He was the quintessential Cold Warrior. For most of his career he was adamantly against any accommodation with the Soviets. He opposed disarmament and nuclear test bans. He was responsible more than any other single public figure for instigating the mania over fallout shelters in the early 1960s. Indeed, it was Rockefeller's machinations at the United Nations conference in 1945 that helped crystallize the postwar tensions between East and West. Later, Rockefeller was asked on a TV news show how long the United States and the Soviet Union could go on not trusting each other. Governor Rockefeller responded, "Oh, I think you can trust them all right. I think you can trust them to try to carry out their stated objective of the domination of the world." It is no exaggeration to say that Rockefeller's views on the Soviets were not terribly different than those of Barry Goldwater or the National Review crowd that reviled him so much. Later in life, Goldwater admitted as much.

Nelson Rockefeller was one of the few people on the American scene who could speak in the same breath of building more H-bombs and fighting smallpox in the Third World. He was a hawk and a humanitarian at one and the same time. This contrast underscores how complex a figure Rockefeller was. Unraveling that complexity and pursuing the contradictions inherent in a man who seemed to be everyone's garrulous, backslapping uncle has kept me busy for years.

He was and is an elusive figure, even for those who worked intimately with him for years. During one of my interviews with his wife, Happy Rockefeller, I asked if she thought that the people who had advised and worked for her husband for years had been well served by them. Her answer was that "they did the best they could with a man they did not fully understand."

I also talked to Oscar Ruebhausen, a man who had been a good friend and legal adviser to Rockefeller for more than a quarter of a century. He told me that "looking at Nelson was like looking up close at an elephant. A lot of us saw a piece of the elephant, and some saw more of the elephant than others. But none of us ever saw the entire elephant."

Rockefeller could be enormously compassionate and caring. In the course of my research I have heard countless stories of how he privately, without any publicity, helped people through personal crises. At the same time, however, he could be thoroughly ruthless in the pursuit of his goals. He could be the most open of personalities, yet he would also display some strange streaks of paranoia. He was thoroughly organized and directed, yet at crucial moments in his career he could often be fatally indecisive.

Among his many contradictions was the contrast between Rocky—the blintz-eating, backslapping politico—and Nelson A. Rockefeller, the lord of Pocantico Hills. Anyone who visits the Rockefeller home at Kykuit—with its Henry Moores and David Smiths on the terraces and lawns, and with that fabulous underground gallery with its Picasso tapestries, its Chagalls, and Warhols—gains some appreciation of the imperial style of the man. Now the property of the National Trust for Historic Preservation, this house is just one of the five homes Rockefeller owned. The other four were the house at Seal Harbor, Maine; the house on Foxhall Road in Washington, D.C.; the duplex in Manhattan; and the hacienda in Venezuela.

Nelson Rockefeller truly projected a kingly aura. Happy Rockefeller tells the story of the time the Earl of Mountbatten, who was the mentor of both Prince Philip and Prince Charles—visited Kykuit. During an argument with Rockefeller, Mountbatten blurted out, "But Your Majesty," before he caught himself.

Like any king, Rockefeller could be supremely out of touch with the day-to-day concerns of the average man. Once during his first year as governor while he was discussing a tax increase with his aides, someone began talking about the effect of that proposed increase on take-home pay. Rockefeller interrupted him and asked, "What is take-home pay?"

There was always more to Nelson Rockefeller than met the eye. Some aspect of the man was always remote and unapproachable. His life was never the open book it sometimes seemed to those who followed his comings and goings in the newspapers, and the manner of his death was equally elusive. Rockefeller's death is often the first, second, and third question people ask when they learn who is the subject of my research and writing. The details of his death, however, will have to wait until I complete volume two of his biography. The only statement I am prepared to make right now on the subject is that like Alice's adventures through the looking glass, nothing was quite what it seemed.

Nelson Rockefeller's life offers many other puzzles, and none greater than the question of how this man, with all of his wealth, gifts, drive, force of personality, and ambition could fail to gain the one prize he sought more than any other: the presidency. With his commanding personality, his mastery of the issues, his vast experience, his tremendous intuitive feel for politics, his incredible force of will, and of course all of his money, how could he have missed becoming president? A close look at the patterns and tendencies in his earlier career provides some insight. Some of the traits and tendencies evident in his earlier life would later prove to be decisive flaws.

One of these traits is what I describe as a sort of strategic blind spot in the man: a failure to see, as he bulls his way toward an objective, the larger consequences of his actions. Time after time, this failing has proven to be the case. In the 1930s when he first become involved in Rockefeller Center, for example, he hired a Mexican artist named Diego Rivera to do the central mural at 30 Rockefeller Plaza. Rivera's devotion to the Communist cause was world renowned. This artist had once done a mural of Henry Ford and J. P. Morgan partaking of a dinner of gold coins and ticker tape. He had also just months before created an uproar with a mural he had done at the Detroit Institute of Art that was denounced as a Communist manifesto. Despite all of these danger signs, however, Nelson Rockefeller hired him to do the Rockefeller Center mural. When Rivera did exactly what would have been expected of him and painted a figure of Lenin into his Rockefeller Center mural, Nelson had to fire him. Rivera's work turned up in trash cans outside the RCA building, and the destruction of Rivera's work became a permanent blight on Nelson's reputation as a patron of modern art.

This pattern showed itself again during World War II. Rockefeller became so caught up with his vision of inter-American unity and in his crusade against communism that he turned a blind eye to the excesses of Juan Perón's regime in Argentina. Through an incredible series of back-room maneuvers and behind-the-scenes machinations, he forced through Argentina's admission to the United Nations. In the process, he almost wrecked the whole U.N. conference, and he humiliated his boss, the secretary of state. He lost his job as assistant secretary of state for Latin America as a result of the uproar. If he had stepped back and considered the longer-term consequences of his actions, much of the damage, particularly to himself, might have been avoided.

Again and again, one can find examples of Nelson Rockefeller seeking short-term victories without fully considering how they might come at the expense of his broader strategic objectives. It brings to mind a comment made by that master political strategist, Otto von Bismarck. "Political genius," he said, "consists of hearing the distant hoofbeat of the horse of history and then hoping to catch the passing horseman by the coattails. The difficulty is one may hear the wrong horse or lunge for the wrong horseman." Nelson Rockefeller's greatest flaw was that all too often, at least on the national political scene, he heard the wrong horse and lunged for the wrong horseman.

Nelson Rockefeller's sheer energy was contagious, infecting those around him. One of his key gubernatorial aides once told me, "Those of us who ended up working with him held him in awe for different reasons. We weren't impressed by the name or the money. What we became impressed with was the man's incredible commitment to what he was doing, and his drive and energy. He was indefatigable. I mean, when most of us were probably half his age and we'd be, you know, pulling our weary bodies across wherever we were going, that guy was still going 90 miles an hour. I mean, it was just unbelievable. And we used to look at him and we'd say, 'where the hell does he get the energy from?'"

That energy really infused his political campaigns in a way that is largely forgotten today. Old-time political reporters told me that the only candidate they ever saw whose campaign could be compared to the energy and gusto of the early Rockefeller campaigns was Bobby Kennedy's in 1969. Moreover, Rockefeller's campaigns had nothing to do with either the money or the name, although they certainly helped to create an aura about him. Rather, his campaigns were about Rockefeller, the man—and in today's times, when most people lack any passion for any of the political candidates on the national stage, it is invigorating to recall a time when such passion did exist.

I will close by sharing a passage from my book that captures some of the excitement and aura that surrounded Nelson Rockefeller. This particular passage is in reference to his first political campaign and successful run for the governorship against Averell Harriman in 1958:

> Meeting FDR for the first time, Winston Churchill once said, was like opening your first bottle of champagne. So it was, as well, with Nelson Rockefeller. His natural exuberance, his zest for life, his contagious joie de vivre were in full flower on the

campaign trail. At Alfred University he popped a blue college beanie on his head to the huzzahs of 2,000 students. In Salamanca he picked up a baton and directed the high school band, then grabbed a Hula-Hoop and tossed it around his neck. At the Rensselaer County Fair he trotted around the racetrack in a sulky, beaming and waving all the while. In Olean he strode into W. T. Grant to pump the hands of astonished shoppers and buy a nickel's worth of green taffy. In Batavia early one morning he shook up the bleary breakfast regulars at Victor's Open Kitchen: bounding in with an ear-to-ear smile, ducking behind the counter to greet the cook, the counterman, the waitresses, and the busboy before joining a table of sleepy Batavians for poached eggs and coffee. "Hello," he introduced himself. "I'm Nelson Rockefeller. I'm running for governor." Appearing at Colgate University, Rockefeller delivered his set speech, then literally leapt off the stage to greet the cheering students. . . .

Rockefeller seemed, for all the world, to have been at the business of politics for years, rather than a mere three months. No one ever had to prompt him to shake hands; he grabbed at every opportunity to wrap his beefy arms around the electorate. (Watching his father go overboard as usual at a country filling station, Steven Rockefeller was heard to mutter, "Let's get him out of here before he starts shaking hands with the gas pumps.") . . .

As a campaigner, Rockefeller had that rarest of gifts: the ability not only to win over the crowd but to completely disarm those he encountered one-on-one. It was the same talent that FDR had, an ability to ensnare every person he met in the force field of his presence. . . .

He applied his solicitude to the humblest of voters. At the opening of the Democrats for Rockefeller headquarters in midtown Manhattan, Rockefeller let the assembled bigwigs cool their heels while he talked for minutes on end with the cleaning woman. When an aide tried to pull him away, Rockefeller snapped, "Just a minute. I haven't finished with this woman yet."

Aboard the Staten Island Ferry one day, Rockefeller assiduously chatted up the bootblack while having his shoes shined. Two days later the man opened his mailbox and found a photo autographed to "to my good friend Tony" and a personal note from Rockefeller inquiring whether Tony might be available to work on his shoes again when the candidate made a return trip to Staten Island the following week. Rockefeller's attentiveness paid off big: it not only swayed Tony but also Tony's many friends in Staten Island's Italian community, which accounted for more than 40 percent of the borough's vote. . . .

In a matter of weeks [Rockefeller] had toured thirty-five of the state's sixty-two counties. In the process he lost six pounds, his palms were heavily callused from shaking as many as 2,000 hands a day, his untrimmed hair curled over his shirt collar (somehow, he couldn't find time for a haircut). Yet at the end of another eighteen-hour day he could still look out over a street-corner gathering of all of fifty people and chirp, "This is terrific. Really wonderful!"—and sound as if he really, truly meant it.

The quintessential event in Rockefeller's first campaign—the event that solidified the image of him, in the media and in the minds of countless New Yorkers, as a hustling, man-of-the-people multimillionaire—was his visit on October 2 to New York City's Lower East Side, in the company of Louis J. Lefkowitz. . . .

Rockefeller . . . had never before set foot in that part of the city, as he readily confessed when he arrived with his son Steven on the appointed day. Despite the pouring rain, the group . . . made its way through the soggy streets. Wearing his by now trademark battered hat and spattered trench coat, Rockefeller waylaid pedestrians and introduced himself. "You're kidding!" one woman gasped.

Then the party headed over to Ratner's, a locally famous Jewish dairy restaurant on Delancey Street. As waiters and startled patrons gathered around, Lefkowitz insisted that Rockefeller try the specialty of the house, cheese blintzes. Biting into one, his first blintz ever, Rockefeller pronounced it "wonderful, absolutely delicious, terrific." As reporters scribbled and photographers flashed, he ambled around the restaurant, autographing waiter's checks, paper napkins, and menus, and advising patrons, "I recommend the blintzes."

The next stop was Max Weitzman's Kosher Delicatessen, a short stroll down Delancey Street. There, Rockefeller munched on a corned beef on rye, donned an apron, posed for pictures with a two-foot salami, and made the acquaintance of a counterman named Ben. Expressing an interest in the salami,

Rockefeller asked Weitzman how much it cost. "Five dollars," the proprietor replied, "but I'll sell it to you wholesale, three dollars." One of Weitzman's regulars was not amused. "For Rockefeller, he gives discounts," the customer grumbled. . . .

The pictures—of Rockefeller toting his two-foot salami, of Rockefeller and Lefkowitz hoisting their corned beef sandwiches—were plastered the next day in newspapers all over the state. Above all, there was the one indelible image: that of the grandson of the world's greatest oil tycoon and son of the world's premier philanthropist happily wolfing down an oozing cheese blintz on Delancey Street. . . .

No longer was he Nelson Rockefeller, scion of Standard Oil. From now on he was Rocky, eater of blintzes. . . .

The reception Rockefeller was getting around the state was rapidly assuming Elvis-like proportions.

In Coney Island, Rockefeller was mobbed by a surging, cheering horde that overwhelmed the four policemen assigned as an escort. Sixteen more officers were summoned to handle the crush. Greeting some of the voters in Spanish, and others in French, Rockefeller inched his way over to Nathan's for a hot dog with Jacob Javits in tow. When Rockefeller emerged from the tumult an hour later, to board a BMT subway back to Manhattan, he proudly bore the scars of battle: rumpled suit, scuffed shoes, mussed hair, and a mustard stain on his jacket sleeve.

In Spanish Harlem five days later, cheers of "Viva Rockefeller" rang out as thousands of Puerto Rican New Yorkers jammed a raucous block party for the Republican candidate. Tossing away his prepared remarks, Rockefeller ad-libbed for twenty minutes in Spanish, pausing only to ask the crowd "*¿ Cómo se dice?*" (How do you say?) when he was at a loss to translate such terms as "seven hundred thousand substandard homes." He promised to hold the line on the fifteen-cent "soobway" fare; when one man shouted out that it should be less, Rockefeller shouted back, "*Mira, hombre* [look man], one thing at a time."

When he was finished Rockefeller vaulted from the stage and was swallowed up by the swaying, dancing crowd. Seconds later he reemerged, hoisted aloft on shoulders like a triumphant matador. "We're losing the candidate. He'll break a leg," one worried assistant groaned. But there was no stopping this

166

jubilant tide, nor the candidate who bobbed along exultantly in their embrace.

A policeman eyeing this scene threw up his hand in disgust. "He's mad, mad, mad," he said.

That was Nelson Rockefeller.   That assuredly is *not* Bill Clinton, Al Gore, or Bob Dole.

QUESTION: It was often reported that Rockefeller's dyslexia made schoolwork difficult for him. How did he cope with that problem? How did he handle voluminous amounts of written material and policy issues? Finally, how would you characterize his own written expression?

MR. REICH: He coped with his dyslexia partly by having his aides write short memos. He was less able to manage his dyslexia in his speeches. As a result, his early speeches were terrible, and even his later speeches were very pedestrian. He was always uncomfortable speaking from a text. When he ad-libbed, he was fabulous, but when he spoke from a text he was always weak. He did amass a great deal of written material, but he often had other people digest it for him. He rarely read books. He once said that the best way to read a book was to talk to the author. As Nelson Rockefeller, he did not have to read the book because he could just call the author, talk to him or her for an hour, and get what he wanted out of the book.

Reading was a struggle for him all of his life. He was not comfortable with it, but he often found ways to adjust.   For example, when looking at long columns of figures, he would find the anomalies by running his finger down the column to feel where the columns jutted in and out. He would then circle the numbers that jutted out and ask about them.

QUESTION: Was Rockefeller with the Department of Health, Education, and Welfare when Arthur Flemming was secretary of the department?

MR. REICH: Rockefeller worked at HEW from 1953 to the end of 1954, but not with Arthur Flemming. The first secretary of the department was Oveta Culp Hobby, but Rockefeller effectively ran the department. Hobby was head of the department in name, but Rockefeller initiated all of the programs, and all of the people reported to him. He was the driving force, not only in the creation of HEW but in its early implementation.

QUESTION: What kind of relationships did Nelson Rockefeller have with his brothers and his children?

MR. REICH: He had complicated relationships with all of them. Of the Rockefeller brothers, Nelson was unquestionably the dominant brother. At the same time, however, his brothers became accomplished, successful people in their own right, and as they became more successful, they chafed at Nelson's domination. Nelson had a close relationship with Laurance, who was in a sense his closest friend. Nelson confided in him and talked to him a great deal about his problems. Between John III and Nelson, there was a politeness, and they worked together on projects like Lincoln Center, but there was nonetheless a certain remoteness about the relationship. As for David, he was the little brother who always got kicked around a bit. Meanwhile, Winthrop detached himself from the family early and was viewed as the errant son for a while before moving to Arkansas, where he became a figure in his own right. He was also distant from Nelson. The only brother with whom Nelson had a close relationship was Laurance.

As far as his own children were concerned, he had a different relationship with the first set than with the second set. The first set grew up when he was moving into his career, and as is often the case with men who are that driven in their early careers, he neglected his children. Though he kept close tabs on them and wanted to manage their lives, he was a distant father and was not home very much. When he did come home it was almost as though Santa Claus or a beloved uncle had come to visit them; there would be an explosion of joy. He had a good relationship with them to some extent, but it was a complicated one.

With his younger children—as is often the case with second marriages—he attempted to atone for past sins. Nelson was much more of a hands-on father with them than he ever was with his older children.

COMMENT: When Queen Wilhelmina of the Netherlands came to visit Albany, Governor Rockefeller was so ashamed of the mall that he decided to build a new one. They called it Rockefeller's folly because he spent so much money on it. In fact, the South Mall could be considered a lasting legacy because it is so beautiful.

MR. REICH: Rockefeller was very good for the City of Albany, although there was a great deal of uproar in the city about his urban renewal plans that would destroy an area known as "The Gut," which Rockefeller viewed as a terrible slum, but which many old-timers in Albany thought was worth saving. In the end, Rockefeller created this enormous edifice at considerable cost. Varying opinions are expressed about the artistic merits of the structure, but it nonetheless reshaped Albany, making the city look like a mecca as opposed to just another old Victorian city.

NARRATOR: It was often said in New York that Nelson Rockefeller never made a mistake while Frank Jamieson was alive, but that Rockefeller made nothing but mistakes after Jamieson's death. Is this conclusion accurate?

MR. REICH: Frank Jamieson's official position was as Rockefeller's public relations person, but he was really much more than that. He was Rockefeller's great counselor. Jamieson's advice was not always good, however. For example, he tried to talk Rockefeller out of the HEW job and the White House job. Jamieson thought that practically every job that Nelson took was a bad idea. Jamieson also tried to talk Rockefeller out of running for governor. Still, Jamieson was a source of great counsel and great wisdom. He was one of the few people who could say no to Nelson Rockefeller and to whom Rockefeller would listen. Jamieson's premature death due to cancer in 1960 created a gap that was never filled for Rockefeller. No one else around Rockefeller could be as abrupt, as rude, or as forceful with him and get away with it. The result was that Nelson was to some extent surrounded by yes-men, some of whom were very capable but nevertheless unable to contradict Rockefeller. Had Jamieson been alive, Rockefeller might not have made some of the mistakes he did later in his career.

NARRATOR: It seems that the Rockefeller brothers developed ways of guarding their turf against Nelson. For example, John Rockefeller III used to tell people at the Rockefeller Foundation that they would be much better off tending to their own affairs rather than dealing much with the brothers. He apparently wanted to guard against any intrusion by Nelson into the Rockefeller Foundation.

MR. REICH: The other brothers always worried about Nelson simply because he was Nelson! Give Nelson an inch, and he would take a mile. From long experience the brothers learned that they could not let Nelson through the door. For example, there was a great uproar when he came back to the family fold in the 1970s after his vice-presidential term because every previous time that he had come back to the family fold after leaving government, he had taken over everything. The other brothers had their appointed posts, but Nelson would demand everything back again. In the past, the other brothers would concede to Nelson, but in the 1970s they finally said no more. Nelson had a rough time accepting their position, and a great deal of internal family struggle occurred as a result.

QUESTION: Was that the reason he took over the Kykuit manor house?

MR. REICH: Kykuit was built for Nelson's grandfather, John D. Rockefeller Sr., by John D. Rockefeller Jr. When John D. Rockefeller Sr. died, John Jr. took over the house. When John Jr. died, the house traditionally would have gone to the firstborn son, but John Rockefeller III did not want it. He did not like the pomp of Kykuit, whereas Nelson loved it. Nelson loved mansions and fabulous houses and was delighted about moving into the Kykuit

170

house. He built another house for his stepmother, Martha Baird Allen Rockefeller, to get her out of the house. Martha was happy not to live in that big old rambling house.

Though Nelson did not do much with the interior of the house, he did transform the exterior and surroundings, remaking it in his own image. For example, he put all of his sculptures around it and included swimming pools and an ice cream parlor for the boys. The swimming pools were filled in after Nelson died and are now two wonderful sunken gardens.

Nelson's taste in art was fabulous. He studied art and learned about it very carefully and had great aesthetic sense. Anyone who visits Kykuit will appreciate how the sculptures have been placed on the grounds, the unexpected ways that things are juxtaposed, the angles, the way they reflect the light, and the way they slope off of the lawn. Both the care and the aesthetic eye that were involved are quite startling. Nelson was also able to mix antique Chinese porcelain with modern art in his house and his apartment and make it work.

QUESTION: When Rockefeller engaged Henry Kissinger as his adviser, was that a first indication that he might run for the presidency?

MR. REICH: Rockefeller's engagement of Kissinger was not an indication of Rockefeller's presidential ambitions. He engaged Henry Kissinger in 1956 to direct the Rockefeller Brothers Fund's Special Studies project, which was created to study and outline a long-term, integrated (diplomatic, economic, and military) strategy for the United States against the Communist threat. Though the creation of the Special Studies project created a national platform for Nelson, his engagement of Kissinger was not specifically directed at a presidential run. Appointing Kissinger to direct the project showed how much Nelson was geared toward big foreign policy efforts and making an impact on foreign policy, and one cannot minimize the effect of Henry Kissinger. Only later did Kissinger become involved in Rockefeller's presidential ambitions.

Interestingly, Kissinger would work for Richard Nixon after Rockefeller lost the 1968 election. As a result of Kissinger's association with Rockefeller, the Nixon people at the outset viewed Kissinger with some suspicion, and to an extent, Kissinger was always viewed as a Nelson Rockefeller man. If Nelson had told Kissinger that he wanted him back, Kissinger would probably have dropped everything to do so. Kissinger was tremendously loyal to Nelson Rockefeller, who paid attention to Kissinger's ideas and made him an important figure. Kissinger recognizes the debt he owes Nelson Rockefeller.

NARRATOR: In which direction did the flattery flow in the Rockefeller-Kissinger relationship?

MR. REICH: It went both ways. I have seen correspondence from Rockefeller to Kissinger in which the flattery was egregious, but Kissinger's letters to Rockefeller were just as bad. Having learned from the master, Kissinger's letters were as oily as Rockefeller's were.

NARRATOR: We appreciate Mr. Reich's in-depth discussion and thank him for sharing his considerable knowledge of Nelson Rockefeller.